WOUNDED
IN THE HOUSE
OF A FRIEND

A BIBLICAL GUIDE TO
OVERCOMING CHURCH HURT

Ronnie Parson

 Broad Wing Press ©

Lanham, MD

Wounded in the House of a Friend
A Biblical Guide to Overcoming Church Hurt

ISBN: 978-1-967034-99-4

Printed in the United States of America

Seymour Press
Lanham, MD

And one shall say unto him, What are these wounds in thine hands? Then he shall answer, Those with which I was wounded in the house of my friends. **Zech 13:6**

Then they cried out to the LORD in their trouble, And He saved them out of their distresses. He sent His word and healed them And delivered them from their destructions.

Ps 107:19-20

A new commandment I give to you, that you love one another; as I have loved you, that you also love one another.

Jn 13:34

Table of Content

APPRECIATION

Special thanks to my wife, Dr. Rubina B. Parson. who is always patient, always loving and always listening.

FOREWORD

This book is exquisite in that it is a much-needed gift to the body of Christ. I am proud to say this book was written by my uncle, Dr. Ronnie L. Parson, Sr. I love this guy! *He is a surrendered vessel whom God is using mightily in Christ's body to respond to His body's needs.* If you seek healing from the distraction of church hurt designed to keep you away from like-minded brothers and sisters, from which you gain strength, *this book is necessary.* It is a source filled with dynamic weaponry(scripture) designed to help you stand, accept adversity for what it is, and mature to a place where you "shall not be moved". *2 Timothy 3:16-17 states,* *"All scripture is given by inspiration of God, and is profitable for doctrine, for reproof, for correction, for instruction in righteousness: That the man of God may be perfect, thoroughly furnished unto all good works."*

In my studies, I've learned that God's word is breathing on us, bringing us life, more abundantly, making us more like Christ. If you are disconnected today and want to return to where you first believed, utilize the tools found in this book to *gird up your loins* so you are ready to withstand this test. Ephesians 6: 14-17 tells us to *"Stand therefore, having your loins girt about with truth, and having on the breastplate of righteousness; And your feet shod with the preparation of the gospel of peace; Above all, taking the shield of faith, wherewith ye shall be able to quench all the fiery darts of the wicked. And take the helmet of salvation, and the sword of the Spirit, which is the word of God."*

Understand you will find yourself in this place where you are faced with this issue because people are people, and our adversary has no new tricks. I can remember a time in my life, many years ago, when I was hurt and very disappointed in one of my leaders in the church. There was a lack of accountability for open sin. Everyone knew what was happening, but it was being ignored. It was as if the messages coming across the pulpit to feed the congregation were for us, and he was exempt. He was living as if those messages did not apply to him.

I was in shambles and very torn. I traveled with this ministry and labored with my whole heart. I have always been very serious about "God's business." I had been a part of the ministry for about six years. I was faithful there every time the church doors opened. I was responsible for the media ministry, among other things. No one made me, and I wanted to! I gave my time and finances and trusted them to cover me and my soul for years! When the sin became an open shame, I was so wounded because I had dedicated my life to the work of that ministry. This ordeal almost made me give up on church, period! In this situation, God showed me where I was in Him. He taught me that my trust needed to be in Him. You can't rely on receiving your every word from God, on which to live, on people, but on me. Psalms 118:8 says, *"It is better to trust in the Lord than to put confidence in man."*

I waited until Sunday morning for them to give me a word from the Lord. Instead of seeking Him for myself, I relied on them. So often, we get caught up in this type of thing and leave the church, blaming someone else. Although I never left God, I did leave that ministry. I was still on the church hurt train, heading nowhere. God loved me enough to show me where I needed to adjust. And so, I did. I spent some time on my feelings because of relationships that were established during my time there. I began to embrace the word of God for myself. **God speaks continually through His word.** His Word is where I found my peace. I began to nurture my relationship with the Lord. I learned to pray for this ministry and allow God to be God. I was not responsible for the type of shepherd he was, but I was responsible for the type of sheep I was. I matured and grew because of this experience. The devil meant it for evil, but my God turned it around for my good. Glory to God!

This book is what the doctor has ordered. It is the answer to someone's prayer. Someone is sitting silently, hurting and alone, waiting for this answer. Praise the Lord. Amen and Hallelujah! You wanted and needed it, so you asked our heavenly Father for it. Well, here it is, yours for the asking. No more excuses! Get up and be about our Father's business. Enjoy your complete benefit package. Don't allow the adversary to deprive you of what belongs to you because of your perception of situations with your brothers and sisters. Choose forgiveness. Fight on, Christians, fight on! Keep your eyes on the prize.

May His love and peace abide with you always,

PREFACE

Since the expression "church hurt" was coined, it has been widely used to describe a variety of very real experiences that have caused mental, emotional, and spiritual injury to individuals who have participated in the life of the institutional church. While acknowledging that the often too familiar experience is real, the Bible lets us know that God has provided mental and emotional healing regardless of the source of the pain. By examining Scripture, we see God's purpose for establishing the church and by seeking biblical-based approaches to addressing injuries that occur within the body of Christ, we can be healed of the wounds that have come about in our lives and help bring healing to others.

Jesus is the head of the church, and the church is His inseparable body. It should not be a place that causes hurt, but bears His name as God-appointed organism for healing and refuge. The church came into existence through the healing power of His sinless body offered as a sacrifice for the sins of the entire world.

Unfortunately, the church has often been a militant institution, used by those who hold our Lord's name in vain to cause injuries to innocent people. From the crusades to witch hunts and torture of innocent victims, and the Ku Klux Klan burning crosses, the catalog of damage in the church's name continues to this day. Cataclysmic occurrences throughout history have undermined God's intention when he purchased the church with His "own blood."

Now the world-wide-web exposes the church's negative to the world. Yet with all the recorded toxicity, our omniscient God created the church as the ambassadors who represent His in a hostile world. Despite its problems, there is God has not removed His church from being His voice in a world filled with many chaotic voices.

A negative psychological message is implicit when the expression church hurt is put into the atmosphere. To say I have car troubles means my car is giving me trouble. To use the term church hurt implies that the church is the root cause of pain. Regardless of the intended meanings, our spoken words are powerful! Though the expression 'church hurt" is heard and understood linguistically, Christologically, and soteriologically, hurt should never be used as an argument against the church.

The church Jesus is building is not the cause of the hurt. It lives through His Spirit and provides for believers in a world that needs to hear the good news. But "hurt" is not one of those offerings. In its over two thousand year history, the Church has never hurt anyone. People within it with unresolved issues, personal agendas, and conflicts are the source of injuries among believers. When those people find their way into leadership, they can abuse authority in ways that may harm innocent. People. However, the church as the body of Christ established by Jesus is harmless. Yet, the institution we call the church often leaves mental and emotional scars that can be buried for years and transcend generations only to resurface later with greater intensity. Yet, blaming the church for the hurt inflicted by individuals feeds into the agenda of the thief who comes to steal, kill, and destroy the bountiful life God intended (Jn. 10:10).

Jesus founded the Church to provide salvation for a perishing world through the power of the Holy Spirit. And the church is the dwelling place of the Holy Spirit and the vehicle through whom Jesus works.

One essential fruit of the Spirit is Love that heals, restores, and empowers. (Gal. 5:22). With the guidance of the Holy Spirit, this book will help us discover how a full recovery from Church hurt is not only possible but promised., Through biblical wisdom, practical steps, and Spirit-led encouragement, you'll learn that even though offenses and disappointments may come, you can walk in a freedom that keeps your heart unshaken.

My sister reminded me that our mother always said, "The word of God has the answers for whatever we need. It's all in the word of God." This wisdom holds true, even when it comes to the pain caused by hurt within the church. Whether you are the one who has been hurt or the one who has caused the hurt, Scripture offers a remedy. The Bible is like God's medicine cabinet, filled with a variety of healing balms—each one a perfect prescription for every symptom and wound brought on by church hurt. (Jer 8:22.)

INTRODUCTION

I was sitting in a Starbucks coffee shop, surrounded by three computer screens. As I began writing this book's final chapter, A pleasant young man approached me and said, "Excuse me, are you a pastor? I said, "Yes." He continued, "I noticed your PowerPoint slide on one of your screens: "Jn 13 to 17." He went on to say that it was one of his favorite passages because it talks about the love that Christ offers. He asked what I was doing, and I told him I was writing the final chapter of my book. When I told him the title, he became excited and said it was a subject that needed to be discussed.

What he said next was interesting. He was a Gen Z; unfortunately, church hurt occurs even in his generation. He went on to say that what is even worse is the general public uses it as an excuse to discredit Christianity in general. I told him that this negative publicity drove me to write this book. At the closing of the twentieth century, self-centered worship was well established. The Faith and Prosperity movements personified *"a Jesus Christ,"* a type of cosmic Santa Claus and Bellhop: one who is at our beck and call as long as we have the excellent faith formula. Anything less than elaborate prosperity, material wealth, and health indicated a lack of faith.

Suffering for any reason at any level was not the will of God. However, Jesus' founder and establishmentarian of the church was clear that offenses are going to come (Matt 18:7), trouble is inevitable (Jn 16:33), bearing one's cross is required for discipleship (Lk 14:27), and being wounded in the house of friends is unavoidable (Zech 3:6) because no servant is more significant than their master (Matt 10:24).

Woe to the world because of offenses! For offenses must come, but woe to that man by whom the offense comes! Matt 18:7

These things I have spoken unto you, that in me ye might have peace. In the world ye shall have tribulation: but be of good cheer; I have overcome the world. Jn 16:33

And whosoever doth not bear his cross, and come after me, cannot be my disciple. Lk 14:27

And one shall say unto him, What are these wounds in thine hands? Then he shall answer, Those with which I was wounded in the house of my friends. Zech 13:6

Yea, mine own familiar friend, in whom I trusted, which did eat of my bread, hath lifted up his heel against me. Psalm 41:9

I speak not of you all: I know whom I have chosen: but that the scripture may be fulfilled, He that eateth bread with me hath lifted up his heel against me. Jn 13:18

Yes, and all who desire to live godly in Christ Jesus will suffer persecution. But evil men and impostors will grow worse and worse, deceiving and being deceived. But you must continue in the things which you have learned and been assured of, knowing from whom you have learned them 2 Tim 3:12-14

All the above can potentially impact the disciples of Christ spiritually, emotionally, and psychologically. But they are part of the cost of discipleship of being in union with

Christ. Wounds from enemies and in the house of friends are both functions of living godly. The church is an institution of salvation and restoration.

> *These things I have spoken to you, that in Me you may have peace. In the world, you will have tribulation; but be of good cheer, I have overcome the world."* Jn 16:33

> *Neither is there salvation in any other: for there are none other names under heaven given among men, whereby we must be saved.* **Acts 4:12**

> *Don't you know that you yourselves are God's temple and that God's Spirit dwells in your midst?* 1 Cor 3:16

> *Now you are the body of Christ, and members individually.* 1 Cor 12:27

The word salvation means safety, rest, and healing. The idea of salvation implies that there are reasons to expect pressure and stressors doing the work of the ministry. Jesus is the head of the church, and the church is His body. He continues to provide healing, rest, and safety for all members of His body.

Meditation for Medication

This book does not suggest that those who have been wounded in Christian service should pretend the injuries did not occur. We must not trivialize the damages that occurred during ministry and tell the injured party to just "pick up the pieces and go on." After almost 40 years in ministry leadership, I discovered that most people who are genuinely hurt while serving Christ are mentally crushed and

3

emotionally fragmented. Scripture calls them the brokenhearted (Lk 4:18), and they often cannot find the *necessary pieces* to continue healthily.

Sometimes, it seems easier to mentally and physically relocate and try to start anew. But, while running away from the source of the hurt may be a temporary fix, it does not get to the root of the problem. It is like putting a bandage on a gunshot wound. The bleeding may stop, but the inward hemorrhaging is slowly killing. Along the way, the injured person usually returns to the crime scene to seek restitution for the missing pieces of their life. Although we may get some appeasement or mental compensation from those who hurt us, the church, the body of Christ, becomes the long-term casualty. The feeling of church hurt originates in lives that have been fragmented and damaged because others who represent Christ are often far from being His ambassadors of reconciliation.

> The Bible, taken as meditation, is a potent medication.

FROM MEDITATION TO MEDICATION

Initially, I grappled with whether the Scripture references should be individual verses or entire passages. I chose to leave the full passages since the whole passage is the medication that will help achieve the needed healing.

Could there be a correlation between spiritual malnutrition and the rise of the cry church hurt? Whether the offender or the offended suffer from inadequate nutrition of the word, I think so.

In 2016, the Barna group analyzed the state of the American Church, looking closely at affiliation, attendance, and practices to determine its overall health Their study found that among professing Christians, 75% pray, 35% attend Church, but only 34% read the Bible (Barna Group, 2016). So it seems that those who want to talk to God (prayer) don't want to hear what God has to say through the *written Word*—God's primary voice. And, as many who do read the Bible use it as an abstract document to support some personal ideology. However, the Word of God has healing properties and provides nutritious supplements for one's soul. When it is consumed, digested, and meditated on, it becomes a potent medication.

Eleven prescriptions from Scripture that serve can be prescriptions that can be applied to the soul to relieve the sense of church hurt and build the immune system of the soul against being affected in the future. Read the passages below slowly and thoughtfully to absorb the medication into your soul. Whether you are a victim of hurt or desire never to be affected, they will help.

There is biblical evidence to support what God has placed in His church to medicate and protect it from being a source of injury and hurt. The scriptures included confirm the heart of God regarding all that concerns us, including the hurts that we feel. Scriptural principles and precepts provide nutrition for spiritual health and medication for injured souls.

From the beginning, God formulated His Word to be the nutritious bread of life that contains healing properties for humanity's soul.

So, He humbled you, allowed you to hunger, and fed you with manna which you did not know nor did your fathers know, that He might make you know that man shall not live by bread alone; but man lives by every word that proceeds from the mouth of the LORD. Deut 8:3

For the word of God to medicate the believer, the believer must meditate on it.

Now when the tempter came to Him, he said, "If You are the Son of God, command that these stones become bread." But He answered and said, "It is written, 'Man shall not live by bread alone, but by every word that proceeds from the mouth of God.' Matt 4:3-4

Then the LORD God said, "Behold, the man has become like one of Us, knowing good and evil; and now, he might stretch out his hand, and take also from the tree of life, and eat, and live forever" Gen 3:22

In the middle of its street, and on either side of the river, was the tree of life, which bore twelve fruits, each tree yielding its fruit every month. The leaves of the tree were for the healing of the nations. Rev 22:2

God created man, a living soul with a body made from the dust of the earth. Because our bodies are earthly, natural food, now called organic food, is the best for our physical bodies, but the word of God is essential for the health of our souls.

So, early in history, God established what would be necessary for a long healthy life for both body and soul. Eating from the Tree of Life was the key to living forever (eternal life). In the culmination of time, the Tree of Life will again be the source of healing and long life. God richly provides His word as the bread of life. So, this book presents scripture themes as nutritious food for thought—the bread of life, meditation for medication, and rehabilitation for the soul with prevention and intervention in mind.

None of this is magic or a matter of *letting go and letting God.* When Israel was causing self-inflicted wounds, the Psalmist reveals that therapeutic properties are in the word of God (Ps. 107:20). Through meditation, the word of God becomes medication. For the word of God to medicate the believer, the believer must meditate on it.

This book of the law shall not depart out of thy mouth; but thou shalt meditate therein day and night, that thou mayest observe to do according to all that is written therein: for then thou shalt make thy way prosperous, and then thou shalt have good success. Josh 1:8

Blessed is the one who does not walk in step with the wicked or stand in the way that sinners take or sit in the company of mockers, but whose delight is in the law of the LORD, and who meditates on his law day and night. That person is like a tree planted by streams of water, which yields its fruit in season and whose leaf does not wither— whatever they do prospers. Ps 1:1-3

Unlimited prosperity awaits those who medicate our souls by meditating on God's law. It is a way of building our spiritual immunity against persistent injury. Vaccinating ourselves against hurt must be intentional. Meditating on the word of God is a deliberate, proactive way to ensure that the health of the soul can withstand slanderous attacks. The Psalmist ties meditating on the word of God with mobilizing to act on the word of God. The blessed one is intentional about how they walk, xxx they stand, and where they sit. Over time, this intentionality yields strength and growth.

A tree planted by water is immune from drought, stagnation, and death. Instead, it does what a soul that is experiencing severe drought due to a lack of meditation on the word of God will be unable to produce spiritual fruit when the season occurs for them to do so. Meditating on the word of God reduces stress and anxiety, both of which cause illnesses and aging and shorten their life: their leaves wither. When meditation is continual, so are the signs of vibrant energy.

There is an essential correlation between meditating on the word of God and doing what the word says to do. Those who do what the word says will discover that their soul's immune system will be strong enough to absorb what would be deemed church hurt. Those who ponder and keep the word of God in their mind will inevitably commit to what the word says (yield fruit). Either they will live by what the word says or risk cognitive dissonance. Something even worse could occur, like having a conscience that can no longer respond to the word of God. To make this point, the Psalmist uses the analogy of a tree planted in a well-watered place that makes it unmovable and thus fulfilling its purpose to bear fruit (Ps. 1:3).

Making a similar point, Jesus uses a well-built house on a rock-solid foundation that is unmovable and able to withstand the worst storms possible.

Therefore whoever hears these sayings of Mine, and does them, I will liken him to a wise man who built his house on the rock: and the rain descended, the floods came, and the winds blew and beat on that house; and it did not fall, for it was founded on the rock. Matt 7:24-25

It gets even worse for those who do not develop a love (appetite) for the truth of God's word. Eventually, they will become delusional, and embrace lies like the truth. The coming of the lawless one is according to the working of Satan, with all power, signs, and lying wonders, and with all unrighteous deception among those who perish, because they did not receive the love of the truth, that they might be saved. And for this reason God will send them strong delusion, that they should believe the lie, that they all may be condemned who did not believe the truth but had pleasure in unrighteousness. 2 Thess 2:9-12

For the Psalmist, a blessed person is watching their behavior through meditating on the word of God. Ultimately, whatever they do prospers, including the successful and proper handling of afflictions. They do it according to truths found in scripture. Our Lord's blessed person is hearing and doing the word of God. No matter what beats on them, they continue to stand and withstand. The storms include any form of offense because their lives are in line with the written word of God. The hurts are not monumental because their faith is on the solid foundation of God's word, which determines their response. To cry, "church hurt," is never a proper response.

I pray that the healing properties in the scriptures presented in this book will do that for all who read and meditate on them, and make them a way of life. Souls aligning their lives with God's word without compromise will be stable enough to withstand any attack framed as church hurt. Hearing and then obeying the word of God over time keeps the soul alive, striving and producing a life that bears fruit. In the Psalmist example, the fruit would be the purpose of one's life. An apple tree grows apples, and an orange tree is to produce oranges. A soul planted in this world is in it for a predestination purpose. That purpose is to be holy and blameless before Christ in love.

Moreover, whom He predestined, these He also called; whom He called, these He also justified; and whom He justified, these He also glorified.''
Rom 8:30

Blessed be the God and Father of our Lord Jesus Christ, who has blessed us with every spiritual blessing in the heavenly places in Christ, just as He chose us in Him before the foundation of the world, that we should be holy and without blame before Him in love, having predestined us to adoption as sons by Jesus Christ to Himself, according to the good pleasure of His will...'' Eph 1:3-5

Staying immune from deep hurt and enjoying a speedy recovery when afflicted are both possible. Not if you are hurt, but when you are hurt! Many are the righteous' afflictions (hurtful situations), but the Lord is committed to the believer's deliverance.

Many are the afflictions of the righteous, But the LORD delivers him out of them all. Psalm 34:19

Then He spoke a parable to them, that men always ought to pray and not lose heart... Lk 18:1

PRAYING THE WORD

So when they heard that, they raised their voice to God with one accord and said: "Lord, You are God, who made heaven and earth and the sea, and all that is in them, who by the mouth of Your servant David have said: 'Why did the nations rage, And the people plot vain things? The kings of the earth took their stand, And the rulers were gathered together Against the LORD and against His Christ.'
Acts 4:24-26

Why do the nations rage, And the people plot a vain thing? The kings of the earth set themselves, And the rulers take counsel together, Against the LORD and against His Anointed, saying, "Let us break Their bonds in pieces And cast away Their cords from us." He who sits in the heavens shall laugh; The LORD shall hold them in derision. Then He shall speak to them in His wrath, And distress them in His deep displeasure. Ps 2:1-5

And they agreed with him, and when they had called for the apostles and beaten them, they commanded that they should not speak in the name of Jesus, and let them go. So they departed from the presence of the council, rejoicing that they were counted worthy to suffer shame for His name. And daily in the temple, and in every house, they did not cease teaching and preaching Jesus as the Christ. Acts 5:40-42

Praying the Word of God is a form of meditation that effectively builds one's strength to endure trials. In Acts 4, Peter and John faced persecution for speaking in the mighty name of Jesus. But they refused to stop. Instead, they came together with their group and prayed, using the Word of God as their guide and encouragement. They continued to spread the message about Jesus. The next time the religious leaders beat them, they were excited to be worthy of suffering shame for his name. Looking at their response shows how far we have deviated from them in how we handle negative responses to our ministry. They prayed Scripture, and when the threat turned into a beating, they were able to rejoice. There is a connection between praying the Word of God and being able to rejoice when suffering.

MEDITATION FOR MEDICATION

PRESCRIPTION 1 - MEDITATION MEDICATION:
PRAY SCRIPTURE AND LIVE BY IT

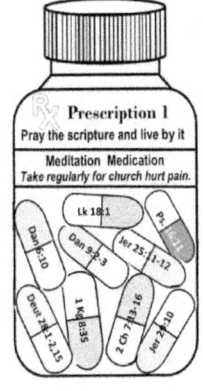

Israel's Covenant Agreement with the Lord

Now it shall come to pass, if you diligently obey the voice of the LORD your God, to observe carefully all His commandments which I command you today, that the LORD your God will set you high above all nations of the earth. And all these blessings shall come upon you and overtake you, because you obey the voice of the LORD your God: Deut 28:1-2

But it shall come to pass, if you do not obey the voice of the LORD your God, to observe carefully all His commandments and His statutes which I command you today, that all these curses will come upon you and overtake you... Deut 28:15

The LORD will change the rain of your land to powder and dust; from the heaven, it shall come down on you until you are destroyed... Deut 28:24

The LORD will bring you and the king whom you set over you to a nation which neither you nor your fathers have known, and there you shall serve other gods--wood and stone... Deut 28:36

Locusts shall consume all your trees and the produce of your land... Deut 28:42

The LORD will bring a nation against you from afar, from the end of the earth, as swift as the eagle flies, a nation whose language you will not understand, Deut 28:49

Solomon Prayed based on the Covenant Agreement

When heaven is shut up, and there is no rain, because they have sinned against thee; **if they pray toward this place,** *and confess thy name, and turn from their sin, when thou afflictest them:* 1 Kings 8:35

God's Response to Solomon:

If I shut up heaven that there be no rain, or if I command the locusts to devour the land, or if I send pestilence among my people; If my people, which are called by my name, shall humble themselves, and pray, and seek my face, and turn from their wicked ways; then will I hear from heaven, and will forgive their sin, and will heal their land. Now mine eyes shall be open, and mine ears attent unto the prayer that is made in this place. For **now have I chosen and sanctified this house, that my name may be there** *forever: and mine eyes and mine heart shall be there perpetually.* 2 Chron 7:13-16

God's word to Jeremiah before judging Israel for breaking the covenant:

And this whole land shall be a desolation and an astonishment, and these nations shall serve the king of Babylon seventy years. 'Then it will come to pass, when seventy years are completed, that I will punish the king of Babylon and that nation, the land of the Chaldeans, for their iniquity,' says the LORD; 'and I will make it a perpetual desolation. Jer 25:11-12

For thus saith the LORD, that after seventy years be accomplished at Babylon I will visit you, and perform my good word toward you, in causing you to return to this place. Jer 29:10

Daniel prayed based on God's words to Solomon and Jeremiah.

Now when Daniel knew that the writing was signed, he went into his house; **and his windows being open in his chamber toward Jerusalem,** *he kneeled upon his knees three times a day, and prayed, and gave thanks before his God, as he did aforetime.* Dan 6:10

In the first year of his reign I Daniel understood by books the number of the years, whereof the word of the LORD came to Jeremiah the prophet, that he would accomplish seventy years in the desolations of Jerusalem. And I set my face unto the Lord God, to seek by prayer and supplications, with fasting, and sackcloth, and ashes: Dan 9:2-3

While in exile, Daniel prayed God's word to Solomon decades earlier. He referenced Solomon's prayer, which he prayed at the Temple dedication: long before the expulsion from Jerusalem and the temple's destruction. God approved of the temple with four stipulations: His people humbling themselves, praying, seeking His face, and turning from wicked ways.

While exiled in Babylon, Daniel's posture of prayer was toward Jerusalem (1 Kg. 8:35) because he is faithful to the prayer that Solomon prayed when he dedicated the temple that the Babylonians destroyed. In the second example, Daniel knew he had been in exile for seventy years and prayed the word of God given to Jeremiah. After seventy years, God would cause them to return to their homeland of Jerusalem.

It is significant to note that they could pray the word of God because they knew it. As God states through the prophet Hosea, God's people who do not know His word still cause much destruction for lack of knowledge about Him and His word (Hos 4:6). In all cases, praying the word of God was the response verses focusing on why they were hurt and who caused the hurt. Jesus Christ is the same yesterday, today, and forever (Heb 13:8). Twenty-first-century believers are baptized in the same spirit that possessed the early church. We, too, can choose to either celebrate for being worthy to suffer for the cause of Christ, or we can blame the church for our hurt. Having a "prayer mind" and a "prayer time" can and will make a difference.

LIVING BY THE WORD

And he spake a parable unto them to the end that they ought always to pray, and not to faint; Lk 18:1

Thou wilt show me the path of life: In thy presence is fulness of joy; In thy right hand there are pleasures for evermore. Ps 16:11

Then he said unto them, Go your way, eat the fat, and drink the sweet, and send portions unto them for whom nothing is prepared: for *this* day *is* holy unto our Lord: neither be ye sorry; for the joy of the LORD is your strength. Neh 8:10

And take the helmet of salvation, and the sword of the Spirit, which is the word of God: with all prayer and supplication praying at all seasons in the Spirit, and watching thereunto in all perseverance and supplication for all the saints, Eph 6:17-18

Therefore whoever hears these sayings of Mine, and does them, I will liken him to a wise man who built his house on the rock: and the rain descended, the floods came, and the winds blew and beat on that house; and it did not fall, for it was founded on the rock. But everyone who hears these sayings of Mine, and does not do them, will be like a foolish man who built his house on the sand: and the rain descended, the floods came, and the winds blew and beat on that house; and it fell. And great was its fall." Matt 7:24-27

But be ye doers of the word, and not hearers only, deceiving your own selves. Jas 1:22

For it is not the hearers of the Law who are just before God, but the doers of the Law will be justified. Rom 2:13

For Jesus to say that one should always pray and not lose heart, is teaching that having a prayer mind is just as critical as having prayer time. Believers should have a set time to pray, but also believers should have a continual consciousness of the presence of God. Always praying is the essence of having an intimate relationship with God.

The Psalmist declares that in His presence, there is fullness of joy, and the right hand symbolizes strength. Later, Nehemiah reminds those rebuilding the wall that the joy of the Lord is our strength. He encouraged them to replace sorrow with the Lord's joy.

Losing the will to continue or faint is a matter of spiritual tenacity and strength. Spiritual muscles are built from doing what the word says to do. Living by the word fortifies one's life against mental and emotional injury and prevents prolonging the damage. Note that the word of God is the sword of the Spirit, not the sword of the preacher or church leader. Apostle Paul knew very well the damage and injury that a sword can cause. In his zeal, he was slaughtering Christians. The word slaughter implies a sword-type object. A knife can be a surgical instrument and a weapon that kills.

Unfortunately, so many individuals were hurt because the word of God was the sword of someone with a personal agenda or ill-informed about the truth of God's word. Jesus, the word made flesh, did not hurt a single soul, neither did he condemn anyone. He said that God did not send his Son into the world to condemn it (Jn 3:16-17). He is our example to follow. Neither has he authorized the church to condemn others.

> For the word of God is living and powerful, and sharper than any two-edged sword, piercing even to the division of soul and spirit, and of joints and marrow, and is a discerner of the thoughts and intents of the heart.
> Heb 4:12

The word of God is a surgical instrument for all who have experienced hurt in the service of our Lord. This is by divine design. The Spirit of God in the servant of God uses the word of God as medicine for a hurt child of God as well as a magnet to draw those who are still alienated from God. At the end of each day, church leaders are workers together with the one who sacrificed his life for the church. As the letter of Hebrews reminds all who place the focus on themselves when they are persecuted:

looking unto Jesus, the author and finisher of our faith, who for the joy that was set before Him endured the cross, despising the shame, and has sat down at the right hand of the throne of God. For consider Him who endured such hostility from sinners against Himself, lest you become weary and discouraged in your souls. You have not yet resisted to bloodshed, striving against sin. Heb 12:2-4

Christ is our example, not other Christians and certainly not celebrity saints. He shed His blood for us while he endured unparalleled hostility. We have not had to shed blood at any time the way Christ did for us. The word of God does not tell us to look around and use people as our example, even though we have worthy examples. But we look up to Jesus so that no one would have an excuse to stay stuck in their pity party of church hurt. Jesus looked beyond those hurting him and embraced the joy that would come from His perseverance. The joy of the Lord is still our strength! Anything less than His joy from abiding in His word and presence is a setup for fainting in the service of the Lord. Christ's response to recognizing the joy set before Him is the example that all believers are to follow. His approach is applicable no matter the source or intensity of the hurt. God is good, and he is constantly weaving good into the evil intentions of others. This message is taught by God through the life of the Patriarch Joseph, a type of our Lord Jesus Christ.

But as for you, you meant evil against me; but God meant it for good, in order to bring it about as it is this day, to save many people alive. Gen 50:20

He came unto his own, and his own received him not. But as many as received him, to them gave the power to become the sons of God, even to them that believe on his name Jn 1:11-12

Our Lord's own rejected Him, causing Him many injuries as Joseph's brothers did to Him. But in the end, their evil acts saved many lives. Joseph experienced insurmountable hurt because of his brothers. But God was with him every step of the way (Gen 39:3, 21, 23). When his master's wife plotted against him, and he spent time in prison, God was with Him (Gen 39:11-21). In the time of trouble, God did not stop the plot against him, but was with Him as the Psalmist said He would be (Ps 91:15). In time, Joseph understood that all the while his brothers hated him and plotted against him; God was planning to do a work through him. The goal was to save more people. When you are hurt in ministry, remember this truth: When you love the Lord and wait patiently on Him, God uses your experience to save more people who are yet to suffer. The Apostle Paul teaches this same principle to the congregation of saints in Rome.

And we know that all things work together for good to those who love God, to those who are the called according to His purpose. For whom He foreknew, He also predestined to be conformed to the image of His Son, that He might be the firstborn among many brethren. Moreover whom He predestined, these He also called; whom He called, these He also justified; and whom He justified, these He also glorified. What then shall we say to these things? If God is for us, who can be against us? Rom 8:28-31

How God anointed Jesus of Nazareth with the Holy Ghost and with power: who went about doing good and healing all that were oppressed of the devil; for God was with him. Acts 10:38

You know how many troubles I have had as a result of my preaching the Good News. You know about all that was done to me while I was visiting Antioch, Iconium, and Lystra, but the Lord delivered me. 2 Tim 3:11

Even today, God is *"bringing good out of evil acts"* in our world, This is one way God deals with all the evil in our world. God is not the cause of evil, but evil does not pose a problem for God. Evil men hurt Christ and had Him crucified, but His death was the best thing for the world in rebellion against our creator! One evil act made everlasting life available to all souls (Jn 3:16). Only God can turn something so horrific and horrendous into something outstanding. The gospel's good news is the Lord's suffering, death, resurrection, and ascension! As my niece says, "Look at God!" So, it does not matter what evil people think or attempt; God's determinate counsel will happen through those who love Him and operate according to His purpose.

No amount of church hurt, or evil dirt thrown on you can stop God from working in your favor. Meditate on this the next time you feel the pain of toxicity in ministry. For those who love God, God's purpose cannot come to a halt by incidents that hurt you. Apostle Paul said to the church, "We know this!" He could have easily said I know, but he said, "We know." Scripture assumes that we know God will not allow anything to turn out bad for those who love Him and are called according to His purpose. However, His loved ones must allow the process to unfold from our salvation to our glorification. We should be intentional about living according to this truth when we experience hurt in the Lord's service. The process is always working in favor of those who love the Lord. Yet, too often, others take advantage of the vulnerabilities that come about because of the wrong choices we make. But God's word is effective medicine, even when the wounds are self-inflicted.

> *Fools, because of their transgression, And because of their iniquities, were afflicted. Their soul abhorred all manner of food, And they drew near to the gates of death. Then they cried out to the LORD in their trouble, And He saved them out of their distresses. He sent His word, healed them, And delivered them from their destructions. Oh, that men would give thanks to the LORD for His goodness, And for His wonderful works to the children of men!* Ps 107:17-21

When the Psalmist exhorts the redeemed to praise the Lord, he reveals yet again the healing purposes of the word of God. Part of working out our salvation in a world that's hostile to Christ is enduring the afflictions that serve to strengthen our faith.

> *Now to Him who is able to do exceedingly abundantly above all that we ask or think, according to the power that works in us, to Him be glory in the church by Christ Jesus to all generations, forever and ever. Amen.* Eph 3:20-21

> *Therefore, my beloved, as you have always obeyed, not as in my presence only, but now much more in my absence, work out your own salvation*

with fear and trembling; for it is God who works in you both to will and to do for His good pleasure. Phil 2:12-13

For whatever is born of God overcomes the world. And this is the victory that has overcome the world--our faith.⁵ Who is he who overcomes the world, but he who believes that Jesus is the Son of God? 1 Jn 5:4-5

CONTESTING THE NOTION OF CHURCH HURT

I have set you an example that you should do as I have done for you. Very truly I tell you, no servant is greater than his master, nor is a messenger greater than the one who sent him. Now that you know these things, you will be blessed if you do them. Jn 13:15-17

Understanding and addressing the notion of church hurt begins with realizing that the church is not a place where our emotions are exempt from harm. When hurting situations arise, believers must count themselves as dead to sin and alive to God. Spiritually this is accomplished by being united with Christ in a mystical connection that infuses the healing properties of His blood in the believer's soul. "With His stripes, we were healed" was the word Apostle Peter used to encourage believers suffering persecution due to their faith in Jesus.

PRESCRIPTION 2 - MEDITATION MEDICATION: *UNITE WITH CHRIST AND ABIDE IN HIM.*

Abide in Me, and I in you. As the branch cannot bear fruit of itself, unless it abides in the vine, neither can you, unless you abide in Me. Jn 15:4*If you abide in Me, and My words abide in you, you will ask what you desire, and it shall be done for you.* Jn 15:7

As the Father loved Me, I also have loved you; abide in My love. Jn 15:9

Who his own self bare our sins in his own body on the tree, that we, being dead to sins, should live unto righteousness: by whose stripes ye were healed. 1 Ptr 2:24

For if we have been united together in the likeness of His death, certainly we also shall be in the likeness of His resurrection, knowing this, that our old man was crucified with Him, that the body of sin might be done away with, that we should no longer be slaves of sin. For he who has died has been freed from sin. Now if we died with Christ, we believe that we shall also live with Him, knowing that Christ, having been raised from the dead, dies no more. Death no longer has dominion over Him. For the death that He died, He died to sin once for all; but the life that He lives, He lives to God. Likewise you also, reckon yourselves to be dead indeed to sin, but alive to God in Christ Jesus our Lord. Rom 6:5-11

[3]For what the *law could not do in that it was weak through the flesh, God did by sending His own Son in the likeness of sinful flesh, on account of sin: He condemned sin in the flesh, that the righteous requirement of the law might be fulfilled in us who do not walk according to the flesh but according to the Spirit.* Rom 8:3-4

To abide in Christ and His love is to be firmly united with Christ. The analogy of the vine and branches is a picture of what it means to be united with Christ. If branches are connected to the vine, they can draw all that is needed to bear fruit. Ultimately the fruit that Jesus is referring to in John 15 is the fruit of love. Those who are in union with Him can draw from Him all that is needed to bear the essential fruit of love. Not the kind of love that is often loosely spoken about in sub-cultures, but the love of God that is only found in Christ Jesus. The love that He demonstrated when He died bearing our sins in His body on a tree.

Jesus condemned sin in the flesh. When it comes to the idea of "church hurt," this is critical to understand because "dead flesh" cannot feel anything! Believers must consider themselves dead to sin and alive to Christ. This is the experience of those united with Christ. Neither can someone with the mind of Christ have psychological and emotional injuries that cannot be healed by the stripes he took. (1 Pe. 2:25; Is. 53:6). The mind that Christ had when He humbled himself to the death of the cross, was made available to the church through the Holy Spirit (Phil. 2). The Holy Spirit is the Spirit of Christ (Rom. 8:9). Therefore, the mind of Christ comes with the Spirit of Christ. But Spirit-filled believers must be intentional in two ways. First, as scripture says, believers must be deliberate and let the mind of Christ determine their response. Reaping the benefits of having the Spirit of Christ and the mind of Christ is neither automatic nor sporadic. It is possible to grieve the Holy Spirit (Eph. 4:30) by not allowing Him to operate freely.

So I say, walk by the Spirit, and you will not gratify the desires of the flesh. For the flesh desires what is contrary to the Spirit, and the Spirit what is contrary to the flesh. They are in conflict with each other, so that you are not to do whatever you want. Gal 5:16-17

I protest by your rejoicing, which I have in Christ Jesus our Lord, I die daily. 1 Cor15:31

Secondly, saints must be intentional about ensuring that their flesh dies and remains dead each day because an internal war rages within all who are spirit-filled. For this, too, God has provided help. God offers more grace to those who humbly submit to His will for their lives (Jas. 4:6). Also, His mercy endures forever. Jeremiah was hurt repeatedly by the people of God. His hurt climaxed as Babylonians trod down Jerusalem, and the elite carried off into exile. Because of this tragedy, Jeremiah spent time lamenting. While lamenting, he had a recall:

> *This I recall to my mind, therefore have I hope. It is of the LORD'S mercies that we are not consumed, because his compassions fail not. They are new every morning: great is thy faithfulness. The LORD is my portion, saith my soul; therefore will I hope in him.* Lam 3:21-24

REDEMPTION BUT NOT EXEMPTION

I want you to know how glad I am that it's me sitting here in this jail and not you. There's a lot of suffering to be entered into in this world— the kind of suffering Christ takes on. I welcome the chance to take my share in the church's part of that suffering. Col 1:24

The infant church of the first century was far from being exempt from persecution: neither did persecution cause a shrink in membership or a slowdown in growth. On the contrary, there was a correlation between persecution, spiritual power, and numerical growth. At the height of the persecution, the church was a powerful church that multiplied (Acts 5:14, 8:1). With the message of redemption being proclaimed, the church grew. I remember an undergraduate professor saying that if the church is not doing Acts 1:8, then the church can expect to see Acts 8:1.

But you shall receive power when the Holy Spirit has come upon you; and you shall be witnesses to Me in Jerusalem, and in all Judea and Samaria, and to the end of the earth." Acts 1:8

Now Saul was consenting to his death. At that time a great persecution arose against the church which was at Jerusalem; and they were all scattered throughout the regions of Judea and Samaria, except the apostles. Acts 8:1

Also, to adequately address the issue of "church hurt," the church as an institution must be distinguished from the church as the body of Christ. The institutional church has a history of suffering and even doing that which caused suffering. But the church that Jesus began on the day of Pentecost must be separated from the historical institution and ideologies that have served to injure so many innocent people. In 2012 I ministered a message at a Church of Our Lord Convocation. I continue to stand by a statement that I made in that message. "If the church is hurting you, it is not God." Furthermore, if something labeled church is killing and oppressing you, it is not affiliated with Jesus. If something is identified as the church condemning you and not redeeming you, it is not the church that Jesus began at Pentecost and had been building throughout history.

For God did not send His Son into the world to condemn the world, but that the world through Him might be saved. Jn 3:17

The thief comes only to steal and kill and destroy; I have come that they may have life and have it to the full. Jn 10:10

Jesus did not come into the world to condemn it, nor did He come into the world to destroy lives. He came to restore God's will to give us life the way God intended: to its fullest extent.

Therefore, the twenty-first century church that emerges as representing the Lord's agenda of offering abundant life is not exempt from suffering persecution. However, redemption saturates the atmosphere and is revealed through the freedom to be all Jesus recreated us to be.

If the Son, therefore, shall make you free, ye shall be free indeed. Jn 8:36

So, believers enjoy redemption from sin, but not an exemption from suffering. Therefore, occasionally enduring being hurt is part of living godly. What we do with that hurt or how we respond to injury in the church can strengthen the church fellowship or further divide it. There is no scriptural guidance for addressing offenses through the idea of church hurt. Scripture teaches us how to guard against and recover from what we label church hurt.

PRESCRIPTION 3 - MEDITATION MEDICATION: *ATTEMPT TO RESOLVE CONFLICTS.*

If we say that we have fellowship with Him, and walk in darkness, we lie and do not practice the truth. But if we walk in the light as He is in the light, we have fellowship with one another, and the blood of Jesus Christ His Son cleanses us from all sin. 1 Jn 1:6-7

Moreover if your brother sins against you, go and tell him his fault between you and him alone. If he hears you, you have gained your brother. But if he will not hear, take with you one or two more, that 'by the mouth of two or three witnesses every word may be established.' And if he refuses to hear them, tell it to the church. But if he refuses even to hear the church, let him be to you like a heathen and a tax collector. Matt 18:15-17

And whenever you stand praying, if you have anything against anyone, forgive him, that your Father in heaven may also forgive you your trespasses. But if you do not forgive, neither will your Father in heaven forgive your trespasses. " Mak11:25-26

Therefore if you bring your gift to the altar, and there remember that your brother has something against you, leave your gift there before the altar, and go your way. First be reconciled to your brother, and then come and offer your gift. Matt 5:23-24

Now whom you forgive anything, I also forgive. For if indeed I have forgiven anything, I have forgiven that one for your sakes in the presence of Christ, lest Satan should take advantage of us; for we are not ignorant of his devices. 2 Cor 2:10-11

Put on the whole armor of God, that you may be able to stand against the wiles of the devil. Eph 6:11

Now all things are of God, who has reconciled us to Himself through Jesus Christ, and has given us the ministry of reconciliation, that is, that God was in Christ reconciling the world to Himself, not imputing their trespasses to them, and has committed to us the word of reconciliation. 2 Cor 5:18-19

If we confess our sins, He is faithful and just to forgive us our sins and to cleanse us from all unrighteousness. 1 Jn 1:9

Confess your trespasses to one another, and pray for one another, that you may be healed. The effective, fervent prayer of a righteous man avails much. Jas 5:16

Who can understand his errors? cleanse thou me from secret faults. Keep back thy servant also from presumptuous sins; let them not have dominion over me: then shall I be upright, and I shall be innocent from the great transgression. Let the words of my mouth, and the meditation of my heart, be acceptable in thy sight, O LORD, my strength, and my redeemer. Ps 19:12-14

To walk in the light is to live according to the written word of God. Living according to the word of God is paramount for maintaining fellowship in the body of Christ. The word of God heals through offering solutions for addressing and resolving conflict between believers in the body of Christ. The blood of Jesus cleanses. Scripture gives specific instructions on how to handle offenses. Those who obey scripture will experience healing and have the church as a mediator for their hurt due to an offense (Matt 18:17). Uninterrupted fellowship is the heartbeat of discipleship. Too often, those who are hurt will find a different church, or worse, leave the Christian faith to join another religion. Or they will become what is referred to as a "none" who claims no religious affiliation. In these cases, the conflict does not find closure.

Scripture teaches that forgiveness, reconciliation, and confessing sin are priorities with God. Unforgiveness hinders praying as well as weakens our defenses against the devil. Those praying, knowing there is an ought with another, must address the concern immediately (Matt 5:23-24, Mk 11:25-26). Being forgiven is tied to one's willingness to forgive those who trespass against them. Unforgiveness is a device of Satan and therefore it gives him an advantage in his relentless determination to devour believers (2 Cor. 2:10-11).

No amount of giving gifts at the altar and offering prayers to God can compensate for the need to remain in fellowship with each other (Matt 5:23). No, we cannot force anyone else to do anything. Still, believers are obligated to do all possible to seek reconciliation and be diligent about keeping the unity of the Spirit in the bond (uniting principle) of peace. Because peace is a uniting principle, scripture says in another place:

> *Pursue peace with all people, and holiness, without which no one will see the Lord: looking carefully lest anyone fall short of the grace of God; lest any root of bitterness springing up cause trouble, and by this many become defiled* Heb 12:14-15

Pursuing peace helps address unresolved hurt that, if left unchecked, might lead to bitterness and cause more trouble. For Christ's sake, we do not want anyone, including ourselves, to fall short of the grace of God! For we must remember that believers are ministers of reconciliation (2 Cor. 5:18-19) commissioned to encourage the unsaved to be reconciled to God. It is the *epitome* of hypocrisy to be a minister of reconciliation while making no effort to reconcile with those who hurt us.

Confession is another to ensure that the hurt caused by those in the body of Christ does not spiral out of control. To confess means "to agree with." When we confess our sins and shortcomings, we agree with God about the offense. The agreement may be simple: "I agree that my presence makes you uncomfortable, but let's talk about it." So much hurt can be dispelled if we seek a better understanding and do not allow assumptions to determine our next move. The devil is a master of distorting the truth and operating in darkness (Eph. 6:11).

Scriptures teach that regardless of the root cause of the aggressor, pursuing reconciliation is the priority. Suppose you remember that someone has something against you. In that case, you must first move toward clearing the air and reconciliation (Matt 5:23). The cleansing medicine of confession comes with a divine guarantee that God is faithful to forgive sin and cleanse us of all unrighteousness. God promises those who acknowledge the sins they know and remember; to cleanse all unrighteousness. What a healer!

The Psalmist David was aware of his propensity to commit willful sins, (Ps. 19:12-14) but we do not always fully understand those errors. The lack of understanding can prevent us from confessing our faults. Yet, there is a link between confession and healing. Confessing to be healed implies that the continual hurt is due to unconfessed sins. Confess your faults one to another and pray for each other. But what if I did nothing but someone did something to me? Confessing faults can still bring about healing. When we confess to be healed, it suggests that ongoing pain may stem from sins or issues we haven't acknowledged. The guidance to "confess your faults to one another and pray for each other" highlights this connection.

But what if you haven't done anything wrong, and instead, someone else has wronged you? Still, sharing your struggles and hurts—confessing your pain—can lead to healing. Confession isn't just about admitting guilt; it's also about opening up, seeking support, and finding restoration through honesty and prayer.

HURT FROM SERVING THE CHURCH

We then, as workers together with Him also plead with you not to receive the grace of God in vain. For He says: "In an acceptable time I have heard you, And in the day of salvation I have helped you." Behold, now is the accepted time; behold, now is the day of salvation. We give no offense in anything, that our ministry may not be blamed. 2 Cor 6:1-3

Incidentally, Apostle Paul wrote this letter partly because he was hurt serving the church at Corinth (more on this later). When a believer is hurt serving the church, regardless of the source, they must keep one critical truth in view. Believers are united with Christ; therefore, they represent Christ and are never alone. The compound expression "workers together with Him" is from the Greek word "synergeo" (transliteration). It means to be a fellow worker and to co-operate with another. It sounds like the English word synergy because synergy comes from the Greek word "synergeo". It can be said that believers synergize with Christ. Believers are energized by Christ's spirit and synergized with Him: united with Christ.

Practically this means that believers are not the primary sufferer; believers suffer with Him (2 Ti. 2:12). Believers are not the primary laborer; believers are co-laborers or co-workers with Jesus. Jesus said that the work of God is that we believe in Him, who was sent by God (Jn. 6:29). Believers must approach difficulties knowing that they are never alone. Being united with Christ, we are in sync with Him, walking to the beat of His drum, energized by the Holy Spirit, and synergized by our union. Those who think about these things will not grapple with hurtful things. Jesus' final words before ascending to glory were, "Lo I am with you always even until the end of the age (world) (Matt 28:29)." Believers are united with Christ; therefore, they are never alone!

Come unto me, all ye that labour and are heavy laden, and I will give you rest. Take my yoke upon you, and learn of me; for I am meek and lowly in heart: and ye shall find rest unto your souls. For my yoke is easy, and my burden is light. Matt 11:28-30

Be anxious for nothing, but in everything by prayer and supplication, with thanksgiving, let your requests be made known to God; and the peace of God, which surpasses all understanding, will guard your hearts and minds through Christ Jesus. Finally, brethren, whatever things are true, whatever things are noble, whatever things are just, whatever things are pure, whatever things are lovely, whatever things are of good report, if there is any virtue and if there is anything praiseworthy--meditate on these things. The things which you learned and received and heard and saw in me, these do, and the God of peace will be with you. Phil 4:6-9

To take on the burden of any form of hurt and carry the load is futile because nothing good or positive can come of it. Instead, Jesus says to bring it to Him and let Him bear it. The combination of labor and heavy laden describes spiritual anxiety and physical fatigue due to emotional exhaustion from overthinking. In this same vein, Apostle Paul teaches believers to think on thoughts that strengthen and restore strength: think on things of virtue (beneficial qualities in Christ) (Phil. 4:8). Virtuous thinking is meditation medication—praying about everything and thinking differently (godly) about everything (Phil. 4:6-9) promises to guard your soul against becoming mentally and emotionally exhausted due to feeling deeply hurt.

Just think realistically for a moment. Can a believer who is united with Christ and walking after the Spirit of Christ be left to bear their hurt alone? Can a believer be alone in their walk with Christ? When said out loud, it sounds like an oxymoron.

The contemporary church must see itself as a continuation of what Christ began when He was on earth and continued to do through the Holy Spirit in the church. Twenty-one centuries later, the church militant continues to survive and thrive with all her bloopers and blunders. Not because it is immune to hurting people who hurt others but because Jesus Christ is the head of the church. He has already done everything necessary to ensure that His persecuted church can remain a powerful church that perseveres to the end (more on this later). He assures His disciples that neither the gates of hell (death) nor persecution would prevail against His church. This book is mainly about how He modeled what it would take for His disciples to represent Him so that the world would know beyond any doubt that believers are His disciples. I will begin with a word from Apostle Peter and then Apostle Paul. Apostle Peter was present for the Passover meal and dinner conversation the night Jesus was betrayed. Peter engaged in the conversation and witnessed what Jesus modeled and taught that night.

Apostle Paul was not present the night Jesus was arrested. However, from glory, Jesus called him into service when he launched a campaign to rid the country of those *of the way (believers)* who first became known as Christians, at Antioch (Acts 11:26). Paul's encounter with Jesus is recorded in Acts 9. More importantly, we learn from his letter to the church at Corinth that somewhere along the way, he received information directly from the Lord concerning that same night.

> *For I have received of the Lord that which also I delivered unto you,*
> *That the Lord Jesus the same night in which he was betrayed took bread:*
> 1 Cor 11:23

Both leaders are examples who followed the Lord's example of suffering without complaining or retaliating against offenders. A brief survey of their thought process can help believers process the experience of being hurt while serving the church.

Another distortion of the truth is to imply that somehow church hurt is a unique hurt that is worse than any other form of mental and emotional discomfort experienced in ministry or life in general. It is different only if we think it is strange and different. Both Paul and Peter, under the inspiration of the Holy Spirit, show the church the proper way to think about and respond to hurts because of persecution. Both address issues where saints experience persecution from the inside and the outside of the church. Also, both agreed that when it comes to being persecuted because of one's faith in Jesus: being hurt serving the church is a welcomed blessing. The experiences are opportunities for receiving new revelations and empirical knowledge (Rom 5:1-2) (Phil 3:10-11). Being united with Christ, they presented a doctrine supported by the example of Jesus. To be in a union with Christ and experience His shame as their own was a source of great joy and desire (Acts 5:41). Apostle Paul desired to "know Him and the power of His resurrection, and the fellowship of His sufferings, being conformed to His death" (Phil. 3:10). Also, Apostle Paul suffered as a prisoner of the Lord. Apostle Peter witnessed how the Lord endured being hurt to birth the church. Both would agree they were blessed to be injured while serving the church. It all feels the same whether the hurt is from inside the church or from a source outside of it.

PAUL: PRISONER OF THE LORD

PRESCRIPTION 4 - MEDITATION MEDICATION: *BE A PRISONER OF THE LORD.*

The next morning some Jews formed a conspiracy and bound themselves with an oath not to eat or drink until they had killed Paul. More than forty men were involved in this plot. They went to the chief priests and the elders and said, "We have taken a solemn oath not to eat anything until we have killed Paul. Acts 23:12-14

Then he fell to the ground, and heard a voice saying to him, "Saul, Saul, why are you persecuting Me?" and he said, "Who are You, Lord?" Then the Lord said, "I am Jesus, whom you are persecuting. It is hard for you to kick against the goads." Acts 9:4-5

But the Lord said unto him, Go thy way: for he (Saul) is a chosen vessel unto me, to bear my name before the Gentiles, and kings, and the children of Israel: For I will shew him how great things he must suffer for my name's sake. Acts 9:15-16

Not that I have already attained, or am already perfected; but I press on, that I may lay hold of that for which Christ Jesus has also laid hold of me. Phil 3:12

*Paul, a **prisoner of Jesus Christ**, and Timothy our brother, unto Philemon our dearly beloved, and fellow laborer,* Phile 1:1

*I, therefore, the **prisoner of the Lord,** beseech you that ye walk worthy of the vocation wherewith ye are called,* Eph 4:1

41

*Pray also for me, that whenever I speak, words may be given me so that I will fearlessly make known the mystery of the gospel, for which **I am an ambassador in chains**. Pray that I may declare it fearlessly, as I should.* Eph 6:19-20

*But I want you to know, brethren, that **the things which happened to me have actually turned out for the furtherance of the gospel,** so that it has become evident to the whole palace guard, and to all the rest, that my chains are in Christ; and most of the brethren in the Lord, having become confident by my chains, are much more bold to speak the word without fear. Some indeed preach Christ even from envy and strife, and some also from good will: ¹⁶ The former preach Christ from selfish ambition, not sincerely, supposing to add affliction to my chains; but the latter out of love, knowing that I am appointed for the defense of the gospel. What then? Only that in every way, whether in pretense or in truth, Christ is preached; and in this I rejoice, yes, and will rejoice.* Phil 1:12-18

And I thank Christ Jesus our Lord, who hath enabled me, for that he counted me faithful, putting me into the ministry; Who was before a blasphemer, and a persecutor, and injurious: but I obtained mercy, because I did it ignorantly in unbelief. And the grace of our Lord was exceeding abundant with faith and love which is in Christ Jesus. This is a faithful saying, and worthy of all acceptation, that Christ Jesus came into the world to save sinners; of whom I am chief. Howbeit for this cause I obtained mercy, that in me first Jesus Christ might shew forth all longsuffering, for a pattern to them which should hereafter believe on him to life everlasting. 1 Tim 1:12-16

The zealous Pharisee Saul converted into Apostle Paul was a Pharisee turned minister of the gospel. He was repeatedly hurt by those he once served with in Judaism and fellow Jews. They went as far as putting a contract out on his life. The attacks continued when he was a militant missionary traveling, preaching, and establishing churches. His ministry began when Jesus used blindness to get his attention. Jesus arrested him on his way to arrest believers in Christ, known then as "those of the way." From the time Jesus changed him from a persecutor of those of the way to a preacher of the way, he was hurt by those who once celebrated and respected him. Once Jesus took him into ministry custody, he saw himself as a prisoner of the Lord. Paul knew that he was sentenced to life in ministry without the possibility of parole. Yet he felt blessed to be arrested because the Lord was his prison ward. The Lord shows Him mercy by putting him into the ministry. He knew he deserved death for what he had done, but because he blasphemed and murdered in ignorance, the Lord had shown him mercy. He was fully aware that he was a mercy case and that the Lord had spared his life to be an example of the mercy of God. But he never forgot how and why he was a minister. The Lord had arrested Him.

For him, the ministry was trying to apprehend why Jesus apprehended him. He suffered greatly for being a prisoner of the Lord. To some in the church at Corinth who hurt him by questioning his apostleship, Apostle Paul gives a comprehensive breakdown of all he encountered in ministry (2 Cor. 11:22-33). Yet when he spent time in prison, he did not blame other people and preachers for coming against him, causing emotional and physical injury. Even in prison, uncertain of his fate, he found solace in knowing the gospel was still being preached. It did not matter that some were doing it to hurt him. His focus was on the importance of the gospel.

> When Satan is not attacking, it's an indication he feels no threat.

The good news kept him from focusing on how he was wrongly accused and mistreated. What a lesson for all believers! The Apostle Paul is in prison with praise, feeling blessed to be arrested because the Lord was His prison ward. Yes, he was in a Roman prison, but he was a prisoner of the Lord. The way he saw his predicament was based on the way he saw Jesus. Because he was a prisoner of the Lord in the custody of Rome, his opposition became an opportunity to spread the gospel of Jesus Christ. We must never forget that the primary reason the church exists is to spread the gospel of Jesus Christ. When the gospel of Jesus Christ is no longer front and center of the church, the church will then be irrelevant. When the church spends more time trying to be relevant to the world, it risks being irrelevant to God. The church at Sardis is the case study for the ministry that was relevant to the world but irrelevant to Christ. Of the seven churches mentioned, it was the only one the devil was not attacking. Like Paul, he endured a considerable amount for the cause of Christ.

When Satan is not attacking, it indicates that he does not see you as a threat to him.

With all the hurt he experienced, Paul continued to fight a good fight and finish His course because he was a prisoner of the Lord. Calling himself a prisoner of the Lord was not a figure of speech or an allegory. He saw himself as a prisoner of the Lord. So, he used his time in prison to write to the congregations in various places. The book of Acts closes with him still under house arrest in Rome. He is using that time as an opportunity to keep spreading the gospel. He is always suffering an infirmity in His flesh due to a messenger of Satan assigned to buffet Him. He prayed for it to disappear, but the Lord refused to remove it. Instead, He reveals that "His grace was sufficient, and his strength was perfect in his weakness." Understanding why he was constantly in physical pain became a reason for him to glory in his infirmity because when he was weak, he was strong.

Suppose more believers today could grasp the importance and magnitude of the ministry of suffering and cross-bearing. There would be no need for church hopping and so much dropping out of the ministry due to being hurt by someone. Can you imagine a scripture canon without the Pauline letters, primarily written from a prison dungeon? Each time he was beaten down and thrown into a dungeon, it was because he was a prisoner of the Lord. Like his Lord, he was never found guilty of committing a crime. Most of his hurt came from others who thought they were serving God, and Paul was in error of the scripture. That would be familiar to Apostle Paul because, ignorantly, He thought those following Christ were committing idolatry and worthy of death.

Paul was a former Pharisee, and most of his hurt came from those he had served beside in ministry. As his Lord before him, he was constantly being hurt in the house of his friends, yet he continued to finish his course. He was keenly aware that the Lord had started the good work in him, and He would perform it until completion. Understanding the Lord's commitment to completion is reason enough for disciples to address any hurt that can potentially stop their forward momentum. Apostle Paul's teachings from prison, while being wrongfully held in prison, confirm that he is practicing what he was preaching. Prison did not stop his biblical instruction, nor did imprisonment stop his praise to God for being his prison, warden.

Being confident of this very thing, that He who has begun a good work in you will complete it until the day of Jesus Christ; Phil 1:6

For these causes the Jews caught me in the temple, and went about to kill me. Having therefore obtained help of God, I continue unto this day, witnessing both to small and great, saying none other things than those which the prophets and Moses did say should come: That Christ should suffer, and that he should be the first that should rise from the dead, and should shew light unto the people, and to the Gentiles. Acts 26:21-23

The apostle Paul was no super saint. He was a man who knew he was a prisoner of the Lord for life because he was a murderer transformed by Jesus into a mercy case, who felt blessed to be arrested by Jesus and to have the Lord as his prison ward. The alternative would have been to have his life ended because he had hurt and destroyed the lives of so many innocent believers. But because he served out His time as a prisoner of the Lord, over 2000 years later, we are blessed by the letters he wrote to churches while imprisoned.

The church throughout history has benefitted immensely from Paul being a prisoner of the Lord because he wrote letters that still instruct the church today on how to do hermeneutics and exegete scriptures. He had to take a Jewish messiah to a Gentile world. He did it by exegeting the bible that he had available to him. The majority of which is in our bible as the Old Testament.

Only the Pauline letters refer to the church as Christ's body. Possibly the day that Jesus arrested him was when Saul realized that the head of the church was in glory, and the body of the church was on earth. He was persecuting the church on earth, but Jesus from Glory asked him why he was persecuting Him. Undoubtedly Saul realized that if he was hurting those of the way on earth, but the Lord in glory was feeling the pain, there must have been a real anatomical connection, a synergy, if you will. Only His letters refer to the church as the body of Christ.

Apostle Paul wrote the letter to the church at Philippi, a small congregation that truly loved and proved it by supporting him while he was in prison. Paul recognized that some ministers were taking advantage of his imprisonment and trying to hurt him. Their self-ambitions and attempts to add more hurt because of his affliction did not cause him to become discouraged with preachers or the church. He focused on what was essential about ministry. It is not my feelings that are protecting my image as a preacher. He rejoiced because the gospel was still going forth. Oh, if the contemporary church can grasp this concept! Not everyone is in the ministry for the right reasons. But the word of God has a life of its own. Therefore, even someone preaching for selfish ambition will participate in spreading the gospel. I'm learning more and more to allow God to judge His servants. Because whether they stand, or fall will be solely left up to him. Even preaching to hurt Paul led to him rejoicing that the gospel was being preached. When believers are Christ-centered, it would be difficult to be hurt by self-centered individuals.

Apostle Paul offered himself to Timothy as an example to follow when responding to persecution in general.

> But thou hast fully known my doctrine, manner of life, purpose, faith, longsuffering, charity, patience, Persecutions, afflictions, which came unto me at Antioch, at Iconium, at Lystra; what persecutions I endured: but out of them all the Lord delivered me. Yea, and all that will live godly in Christ Jesus shall suffer persecution. But evil men and seducers shall wax worse and worse, deceiving, and being deceived. 2 Tim 3:10-13

For Paul, the persecution he experienced as a believer was part of his determination to live godly. All who make living godly their goal must brace themselves for nonstop persecution. Believers should expect evildoers and seducers (imposters) to go from bad to worse.

For I know this, that after my departing shall grievous wolves enter in among you, not sparing the flock. Also of your own selves shall men arise, speaking perverse things, to draw away disciples after them. Acts 20:29-30

Before going to Jerusalem to never see them again, Apostle Paul warns the congregation at Ephesus concerning outsiders and insiders. Outsiders acting like grievous wolves will come in and not spare the flock of God. Also, some would arise among the church, speaking things that distort the truth, drawing away disciples after them. Church history is filled with those who did just that, even in recent church history. Everything from Mormonism to James Warren Jones (Jim Jones), a professing preacher who led almost a thousand away to their death by drinking poison.

Apostle Paul shares with his spiritual son, Timothy, that the last days would usher in difficult times. The times would be characterized by those who have a form of godliness but will deny the power of godliness. Among other things, people would be lovers of themselves, without natural affection, despisers of those that are good, and lovers of pleasure more than lovers of God. A form of godliness without the power of godliness is a formula for hurting innocent and straightforward people who love the Lord and desire to do what is right. Those in authority will inevitably hurt people in the church who love themselves more than they love God.

It is important to note that the first-century church believers, our apostolic mothers, and fathers, fully understood that being hurt by others among them was not caused by the church. Yes, they faced intense persecution from outsiders, but there were insiders as well, doing emotional damage that would fall in the category of what is now being referred to as church hurt.

The church at Corinth that Apostle Paul founded on one of his missionary journeys had some members who hurt him deeply. They questioned his apostleship and were embarrassed to associate with him. Mainly because he lived a simple life that often meant poverty; he was homeless at times and constantly experiencing some form of hardship. He was hurt by them when some suggested that he show some credentials to validate his apostleship. To this, he responds recorded in our second Corinthians (most likely the third letter):

> *Do we begin again to commend ourselves? Or do we need, as some others, epistles of commendation to you or letters of commendation from you? ²* *You are our epistle written in our hearts, known and read by all men; ³* *clearly you are an epistle of Christ, ministered by us, written not with ink but by the Spirit of the living God, not on tablets of stone but on tablets of flesh, that is, of the heart.* 2 Cor 3:1-3

The reader can feel his hurt as he refers to passages from Jeremiah and Ezekiel (verse 3) highlighting Judah's sins. Sins that caused God to finally announce that He would write no longer on stones but on their hearts by the Spirit of God: so that they would have the power to be obedient to His word and love Him the way He desired to be loved.

And I will give them one heart, and I will put a new spirit within you; and I will take the stony heart out of their flesh, and will give them an heart of flesh: Ezk 11:19

A new heart also will I give you, and a new spirit will I put within you: and I will take away the stony heart out of your flesh, and I will give you an heart of flesh. And I will put my spirit within you, and cause you to walk in my statutes, and ye shall keep my judgments, and do them. Ezk 36:26-27

The sin of Judah is written with a pen of iron, and with the point of a diamond: it is graven upon the table of their heart, and upon the horns of your altars Jer 17:1

The reader experiences Apostle Paul's deep disappointment with those he birthed into the body of Christ. He was hurt by their questioning his credentials as an Apostle. He responded that they, the saints at Corinth were his credentials!

who also made us sufficient as ministers of the new covenant, not of the letter but of the Spirit; for the letter kills, but the Spirit gives life. 2 Cor 3:6

Also, there were members in the church at Corinth that other members in the ministry were hurting. A man was having sexual relations with his father's wife, and other members thought his behavior was acceptable (1 Cor. 5:1-2). Others were taking each other to court. To this, Apostle Paul instructed them to handle these matters among themselves and not go before unjust judges. Church members will have disagreements, but to maintain and protect the name of Jesus, we must resolve those matters among ourselves (1 Cor. 6:1-8). Also, some husbands and wives hurt each other by defrauding each other. To this, the Apostle Paul taught them to fulfill their marital duties to each other (1 Cor. 7).

Some in this church were flaunting their freedom related to dietary laws. They were intentionally hurting those who were vehemently in opposition. To this, Apostle Paul advised:

> *Christ gave up his life for that person. Wouldn't you at least be willing to give up going to dinner for him—because, as you say, it doesn't really make any difference? But it does make a difference if you hurt your friend terribly, risking his eternal ruin! When you hurt your friend, you hurt Christ. A free meal here and there isn't worth it at the cost of even one of these "weak ones."* 1 Cor 8:11-12 (MSG)

Being hurt by other church members is a reason to teach about true love, not a reason to focus on the hurt that only leads to more division in the body of Christ. Later in the same letter, Apostle Paul addressed dissension surrounding an agape feast that included communion at some point.

> *So then, when you come together, it is not the Lord's Supper you eat, [21] for when you are eating, some of you go ahead with your own private*

suppers. As a result, one person remains hungry and another gets drunk. Don't you have homes to eat and drink in? Or do you despise the church of God by humiliating those who have nothing? What shall I say to you? Shall I praise you? Certainly not in this matter! 1 Cor 11:20-22

Some members were disrespected even shaming others by their self-centered behavior. To deal with this hurt their pastor focused on "the why" of communion.

For whenever you eat this bread and drink this cup, you proclaim the Lord's death until he comes. 1 Cor 11:26

Communion is a remembrance of the Lord's death that gave life to the church—the body of Christ. Christ is one body of many members working together, loving and supporting each other, and bringing glory to the name of the Lord Jesus. Imagine if the hurt members would have left the congregation. The knowledge of the dispute would have spread, further undermining the church's message. No, they gave their pastor a chance to deal with it.

PETER EYEWITNESS AND LEAD DISCIPLE

Forasmuch then as Christ hath suffered for us in the flesh, arm yourselves likewise with the same mind: for he that hath suffered in the flesh hath ceased from sin; 1 Ptr 4:1

Here Peter is telling Gentile believers who are hurting because of persecution to use Jesus as their example. Peter being an eyewitness of Jesus enduring physical, mental, emotional, and spiritual hurt, encourages saints under persecution to arm themselves likewise. I suspect that years later, after the night.

PRESCRIPTION 5 - MEDITATION MEDICATION: *ACCEPT GOD'S WILL AS THE ONLY WAY TO EXPERIENCE HURT.*

Ye men of Israel, hear these words; Jesus of Nazareth, a man approved of God among you by miracles and wonders and signs, which God did by him in the midst of you, as ye yourselves also know: Him, being delivered by the determinate counsel and foreknowledge of God, ye have taken, and by wicked hands have crucified and slain: Acts 2:22-23

When He came to the place, He said to them, "Pray that you may not enter into temptation." And He was withdrawn from them about a stone's throw, and He knelt down and prayed, saying, "Father, if it is Your will, take this cup away from Me; nevertheless not My will, but Yours, be done." Then an angel appeared to Him from heaven, strengthening Him. And being in agony, He prayed more earnestly. Then His sweat became like great drops of blood falling down to the ground. When He rose up from prayer, and had come to His disciples, He found them sleeping from sorrow. Then He said to them, "Why do you sleep? Rise and pray, lest you enter into temptation." Lk 22: 40-46

Then Simon Peter having a sword drew it, and smote the high priest's servant, and cut off his right ear. The servant's name was Malchus. Then said Jesus unto Peter, put up thy sword into the sheath: the cup which my Father hath given me, shall I not drink it? Jn 18:10-11

And one of them struck the servant of the high priest and cut off his right ear. But Jesus answered and said, "Permit even this." And He touched his ear and healed him. Then Jesus said to the chief priests, captains of the temple, and the elders who had come to Him, "Have you come out, as against a robber, with swords and clubs? [53] When I was with you daily in the temple, you did not try to seize Me. But this is your hour, and the power of darkness." Lk 22:50-53

[52] But Jesus said to him, "Put your sword in its place, for all who take the sword will perish by the sword. [53] Or do you think that I cannot now pray to My Father, and He will provide Me with more than twelve legions of angels? [54] How then could the Scriptures be fulfilled, that it must happen thus?" Matt 26:52-54

looking unto Jesus, the author and finisher of our faith, who for the joy that was set before Him endured the cross, despising the shame, and has sat down at the right hand of the throne of God. Heb 12:2

Rejoice always, pray without ceasing, in everything give thanks; for this is the will of God in Christ Jesus for you. Do not quench the Spirit. 1 Thess 5:16-19

Jesus is the believer's example that accepting the will of God is the only way to experience unnecessary pain and hurt. The suffering death of Jesus was the determinate counsel of God (Acts 2:23). The source of His hurt was from those who professed to be the people of God. The night Jesus willfully allowed Himself to go into the custody of evil men, Peter was armed with a sword, ready to fight and die if that was what it took to defend Jesus. So, when Jesus was under siege, Peter used his sword and cut off the ear of one of the servants of the Chief Priest. After agonizing over the coming suffering, Jesus accepted the will of God that would entail much physical, mental, and emotional pain.

In a post-Pentecostal discourse, Peter reminded the religious leaders that they led the way in carrying out the heinous act within the boundaries of what God had determined should be done. Instead of engaging in the fight, Jesus stopped Peter and healed the man with his ear severed by Peter's sword. He healed one of those who came to hurt Him. Two more things worth mentioning. The Chief Priests (and High Priest) played a lead role in the decision to put Jesus to death (Matt 27:1), carry out the betrayal negotiation with Judas (Matt 27:3-6), arrest Jesus (Mk 14:47, Lk 22:50), the questioning, getting false witnesses, the accusations against Jesus at the trial (Matt 27:12), stirring up the crowd to choose to release Barabbas over Jesus (Matt 27:20), as well as the devil using their mouth at the crucifixion of Jesus: taunting him to come down if he was the son of God (Matt 27:41). This expression was right from the devil's playbook when he tempted Jesus in the wilderness at the beginning of His ministry: if you are the son of God command stones to be turned into bread (Matt 4:3). The Chief Priests said to Pilate that they had no king but Caesar (Jn. 19:15). Those who were to hold God in High esteem as their king stooped to the level of identifying Caesar as their king. Above is a graphical summary of how much the haters of Jesus were bent on hurting and humiliating him. Peter was an eyewitness; this was the example he put before believers struggling with being persecuted as Christians.

> *But how is it to your credit if you receive a beating for doing wrong and endure it? But if you suffer for doing good and you endure it, this is commendable before God. To this you were called, because Christ suffered for you, leaving you an example, that you should follow in his steps. "He committed no sin, and no deceit was found in his mouth." When they hurled their insults at him, he did not retaliate; when he suffered, he made no threats. Instead, he entrusted himself to him who judges justly. "He himself bore our sins" in his body on the cross, so that we might die to sins and live for righteousness; "by his wounds you have been healed." For "you were like sheep going astray," but now you have returned to the Shepherd and Overseer of your souls.* 1 Ptr 2:20-25

The second thing worth mentioning is that all three synoptic gospels, as well as John, record the incident of Peter cutting off the ear of the servant of the Chief Priest the night Jesus began to accomplish death (Matt 26:51, Mk 14:47, Lk

22:50, Jn18.10) They all knew that somebody did it. Lk mentions it was the right ear, and Jesus touched his ear and healed him. It is unclear whether Jesus uses the same ear or creates a new one. Also, only John records that Peter cut off the ear. John also names Malchus as the high priest's servant who lost an ear reattached by Jesus (Jn 18:10). Although the gospels were written years later, the Holy Spirit ensured that no one forgot this historical moment. All recorded the moment Jesus stops a fight from spiraling into unrest and bloodshed. Jesus had already determined that the only bloodshed that night would be His own. The Passover meal transformed into a new covenant-making meal: "This is my blood that is shed for you" (Lk 22:20)! Lord, I love you!

Peter's action suggests that arresting Jesus was an explicit declaration of a fight to the finish. Peter had drawn first blood. What would Jesus do? Whatever Jesus is going to do, He must do it quickly! Soldiers are there, and they know how to neutralize a threat swiftly and precisely. Would Jesus stop it, or would He endorse it? The mob, including soldiers, was no match for the host of angels mobilized to help Jesus. The angels were there before the mob arrived to arrest Jesus. Earlier, an angel was already in the area to strengthen Jesus as He was in agony, sweating drops of blood and pleading for His Father to remove the cup (Lk 22:43). At that moment, more than twelve legions (more than 72,000) of angels were just one prayer away, waiting for Jesus to either change His mind and fight not to be arrested or choose to go through a horrendous process of taking away all the sins of the world. With all history hanging in the balance and the fate of humanity hanging on one decision: will Jesus go through with suffering, or will he change His mind?

Just before the mob arrived, Jesus had already decided that as much as He was not looking forward to the brutality that was on the horizon, nothing would stop Him from carrying out His Father's will: to be the lamb of God to take away the sins of the world (Lk 22:22, Jn 1:36). This alone is incomprehensible when one considers the hurt, he would experience. Even though He despised the shame, the joy that awaited Him for doing the will of God was more than worth the experience. What a mighty God we serve! It is almost a travesty to think that Jesus went through all of this for us, and believers tend to maximize what occurs when hurt doing what He commissioned us to do. Jesus took all the pain so that we could have the power to take hurt that is always far less than His suffering. We have yet to shed blood for others as He did for the world.

Also, Jesus had warned Peter to watch and pray because without it, entering temptation was inevitable (Lk 22:40). But Peter, James, and John were too exhausted to stay awake. Their spirit was willing, but their flesh was weak (Matt 26:41). Just as Jesus had warned them: when the mob came, Peter entered the temptation to fight and risk much bloodshed, something that the devil would have welcomed. Jesus stopped what could and would have been a blood bath. Had Jesus prayed for the twelve legions of angels, the scene would have been catastrophic. Especially when considering that in one night, one angel "killed in the camp of the Assyrians one hundred and eighty-five thousand; and when people arose early in the morning, there were the corpses—all dead (Isa 37:36).

Imagine how much damage twelve legions would have done if the Word that created them had summoned them to His aide. Jesus cemented that decision when he touched the side of Malchus's head and healed his ear. Peter cut off the ear. Nothing suggests that Jesus picked up the ear and reattached it. The text suggests that Jesus created another ear in the place of it. What did Malchus think when he stopped hurting because he received a new ear? If he was married with children, what did he tell them when he went home that night? Did he take part in the beating of Jesus after being healed by Jesus? We will never know, but these questions are food for thought. Especially when this is put in the context of what it sounds like to say, *church and hurt* together as a compound expression.

The man who healed the ear hurt, stopping days of physical pain, is the same man who established the church with His resurrection power. He healed one man's hurt the same night he was betrayed, arrested, denied, emotionally taunted, and brutally mistreated. The creator of the church stopped the hurt of one who took part in arresting Him. Jesus refused to allow any of his enemies or His disciples to be hurt the night He was taken and inhumanely mistreated—the night when the power of darkness was about to be released on Him in all its fury.

To reminisce on this scene is breathtaking to me. Jesus is helping those who are just minutes from hurting Him in ways that are still unimaginable. Jesus knows very well what they were about to do to Him, but he moves swiftly to stop the physical pain of one of His arresting officers. In the process, he stops a cataclysmic war between over seventy-two thousand angels and soldiers who were no match for them. Just thinking about this alone should remove any desire for a believer to connect the church with hurt. The church belongs to this man who would not even allow those who would inflict pain on Him to suffer pain while arresting Him.

After having a chance to process and reflect on it, Peter realized that Jesus was armed to carry out the will of God, and his sword was not needed to support Jesus. Jesus didn't need a sword that night. He was armed with the right frame of mind. What occurred that night is not one of those things that a person could easily forget. He witnessed how Jesus responded to being hurt, and he encouraged the church to model His behavior.

Peter further teaches the hurting church members being persecuted not to think that their suffering is unusual. Whether the source is due to wolves in sheep's clothing, ministers of Satan transformed as angels of light, or sinful flesh refusing to die and remain dead, being hurt and holy are inseparable. This book uses the conversation that Jesus had with his disciples to guide how to avoid church hurt and overcome or recover from church hurt. It is a Christological approach versus a psychological approach.

> *But ye are a chosen generation, a royal priesthood, an holy nation, a peculiar people; that ye should shew forth the praises of him who hath called you out of darkness into his marvellous light:* 1 Ptr 2:9

Being a holy people of God, the way Scripture defines holy, is a magnet for injury from others. Peter's audience was Gentile or non-Jewish Christians facing suffering and hostility from their neighbors.

> *Shepherd the flock of God which is among you, serving as overseers, not by compulsion but willingly, not for dishonest gain but eagerly; nor as being lords over those entrusted to you, but being examples to the flock;* 1 Ptr 5:2-3

For Peter to instruct overseers to feed the flock of God, not for dishonest gain, suggests that the infant church was already vulnerable to lousy leadership that would take advantage of the congregation.

Someone may say that church hurt focuses mainly on how church leaders injure church members. To this, I say that every shepherd is a sheep of the Lord's pasture (Ps. 100:3). The only difference is that he was a lead sheep for the Lord's sheep. David writes about this in Psalm 23 when he begins by saying The Lord is my shepherd, and I shall not want (v1). Besides our Lord, David was the most excellent known shepherd of the Lord's people. David says, "Surely goodness and mercy shall follow me all the days of my life" (v6).

Shepherds tend to designate and train a lead sheep. The lead sheep is so proficient that the shepherd can lead from behind while the lead sheep leads the flock. I cannot psychoanalyze David's mind from a distance or say what was on his mind: but it could be that David is saying that the Lord designated him as a lead sheep. A lead sheep is fully confident that the Lord's goodness and mercy are still leading him from the rear: goodness and mercy are following him all the days of his life.

At the time he wrote this Psalm, David was of significant age. He is looking back on His experiences with the Lord as his shepherd (he is a sheep), but he had been a shepherd of the Lord's people. Every shepherd is a lead sheep of the Lord's people; therefore, shepherds are also vulnerable to being hurt. I know this truth very well as a sheep (believer) and shepherd (pastor).

PERSISTENT HURTING: LUSTING TO THE END

But put ye on the Lord Jesus Christ, and make not provision for the flesh, to fulfil the lusts thereof. Rom 13:14

For all that *is* in the world--the lust of the flesh, the lust of the eyes, and the pride of life--is not of the Father but is of the world. 1 Jn 2:16

For all the law is fulfilled in one word, even in this: "You shall love your neighbor as yourself." But if you bite and devour one another, beware lest you be consumed by one another! [16] *I say then: Walk in the Spirit, and you shall not fulfill the lust of the flesh. For the flesh lusts against the Spirit, and the Spirit against the flesh; and these are contrary to one another, so that you do not do the things that you wish.* Gal 5:14-17

And they that are Christ's have crucified the flesh with the affections and lusts. Gal 5:24

But if ye bite and devour one another, take heed that ye be not consumed one of another. This I say then, Walk in the Spirit, and ye shall not fulfil the lust of the flesh. For the flesh lusteth against the Spirit, and the Spirit against the flesh: and these are contrary the one to the other: so that ye cannot do the things that ye would. But if ye be led of the Spirit, ye are not under the law. Gal 5:15-18

In English, the word 'lust' usually has sexual connotations. But the biblical word translated lust is a longing and a desire, especially for something forbidden. Inherent in our sinful DNA is the longing to highlight our struggles, protect our feelings, and retaliate against those who injure us. It is natural for us to make accommodations to protect ourselves. So, it goes against the grain of being human to say, "make no provisions for the flesh." "Do not fulfill the desires of the flesh." "Crucify the flesh." At the time of Jesus, crucifixion was the most gruesome and painful death known to man. His flesh was full of wounds and stripes; the trauma to His senses would have been immeasurable, and the mental stresses incomprehensible.

Scripture teaches us to deny our flesh if it must suffer the most painful death possible; Jesus is our model. He is the only human who knows the depth of suffering without His own sins. In this way, as the prophet Isaiah foresaw, "His countenance would have been worse than any other human (Is. 52:14))." As the church fills up the afflictions He left behind (Col. 1:24), every believer must do whatever is necessary to ensure that longing for desires does not make the will of God null and void. Suffering to obey the word of God is always a teaching moment. Theologically, I can't say for sure why this is the case, but I do know that Adam learned obedience the hard and suffering way. He may have set the standard for a history of being taught obedience cruelly. Jesus, the second man Adam, showed new creation believers how it's done.

who, in the days of His flesh, when He had offered up prayers and supplications, with vehement cries and tears to Him who was able to save Him from death, and was heard because of His godly fear, though He was a Son, yet He learned obedience by the things which He suffered.
Heb 5:7-8

God has no intention of freeing our physical flesh from every hurt we encounter. Instead, being united with him allows his mindset to determine how we respond to sin and suffering that tries to rule our bodies and suffer for Christ's transformational cause. Suffering and cross-bearing are critical aspects of being united with Christ. Regarding how Christians are hurt, being wronged, and hurt is a part of being a follower of Jesus.

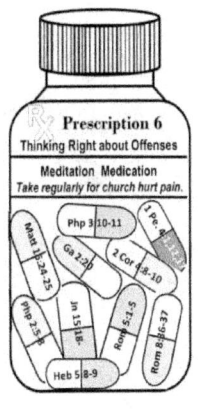

Let this mind be in you, which was also in Christ Jesus Who, being in the form of God, thought it not robbery to be equal with God: But made himself of no reputation, and took upon him the form of a servant, and was made in the likeness of men: And being found in fashion as a man, he humbled himself, and became obedient unto death, even the death of the cross. Phil 2:5-8

If the world hates you, you know that it hated Me before it hated you. If you were of the world, the world would love its own. Yet because you are not of the world, but I chose you out of the world, therefore the world hates you. Remember the word that I said to you, 'A servant is not greater than his master.' If they persecuted Me, they will also persecute you. If they kept My word, they will keep yours also. But all these things they will do to you for My name's sake, because they do not know Him who sent Me. Jn 15:18-21

Then said Jesus unto his disciples, If any man will come after me, let him deny himself, and take up his cross, and follow me. For whosoever will save his life shall lose it: and whosoever will lose his life for my sake shall find it. Matt 16:24-25

Therefore, having been justified by faith, we have peace with God through our Lord Jesus Christ, through whom also we have access by faith into this grace in which we stand, and rejoice in hope of the glory of God. And not only that, but we also glory in tribulations, knowing that tribulation produces perseverance; and perseverance, character; and character, hope. Now hope does not disappoint, because the love of God has been poured out in our hearts by the Holy Spirit who was given to us. Rom 5:1-5

Yea, for thy sake are we killed all the day long; we are counted as sheep for the slaughter. Ps. 44:22 [37]

Who shall separate us from the love of Christ? shall tribulation, or distress, or persecution, or famine, or nakedness, or peril, or sword? [3] *As it is written, For thy sake we are killed all the day long; we are accounted as sheep for the slaughter* Romans 8:35-36

Nay, in all these things we are more than conquerors through him that loved us. Rom 8:37

I am crucified with Christ: nevertheless I live; yet not I, but Christ liveth in me: and the life which I now live in the flesh I live by the faith of the Son of God, who loved me, and gave himself for me. Gal 2:20

We are troubled on every side, yet not distressed; we are perplexed, but not in despair; Persecuted, but not forsaken; cast down, but not destroyed; Always bearing about in the body the dying of the Lord Jesus, that the life also of Jesus might be made manifest in our body. 2 Cor 4:8-10

that I may know Him and the power of His resurrection, and the fellowship of His sufferings, being conformed to His death, if, by any means, I may attain to the resurrection from the dead. Phil 3:10-11

Forasmuch then as Christ hath suffered for us in the flesh, arm yourselves likewise with the same mind: for he that hath suffered in the flesh hath ceased from sin 1 Ptr 4:1

Though he were a Son, yet learned he obedience by the things which he suffered; And being made perfect, he became the author of eternal salvation unto all them that obey him Heb 5:8-9

Beloved, think it not strange concerning the fiery trials which is to try you, as though some strange thing happened unto you: But rejoice, inasmuch as ye are partakers of Christ's sufferings; that, when his glory shall be revealed, ye may be glad also with exceeding joy... But let none of you suffer as a murderer, or as a thief, or as an evildoer, or as a busybody in other men's matters. Yet if any man suffer as a Christian, let him not be ashamed; but let him glorify God on this behalf. For the time is come that judgment must begin at the house of God: and if it first begin at us, what shall the end be of them that obey not the gospel of God? 1 Ptr 4:12 -17

The above medication goes right to the mindset at the heart of our thoughts that exacerbates the idea of being wronged by another believer in the body of Christ and those outside the body of Christ. Thinking right about being wronged by others begins with considering the thoughts of Christ when he suffered to bring salvation to the entire world. The medication above is highly effective when the hurt diagnosis is from symptoms due to suffering as a Christian. For prescriptions due to suffering from making bad choices, etc., see *Prescription 6*. When the sufferer is feeling pain and pressure due to being faithful to cross-bearing, this meditation medication is highly effective: *"thinking right about being wronged,"*

Thinking right about being wronged may be a tough pill to swallow. But those who can take it will feel much better about being hurt while engaged in ministry. Also, the medicine gets to the root of why believers can continue to experience persistent hurt when they are wronged by others, especially by those who are within the same household of faith (Gal. 6:10). It is usual for our flesh to lust to protect itself from all suffering and hurt. However, when the hurt is from being who the Lord saved you to be, persistent hurting is mainly due to thoughts about trials and trouble. Scripture instructs us to adjust our mindset to be set on the experience of our Lord. He endured suffering in the flesh to death on the cross, and eventually, His suffering ceased. The benefits of His suffering did not stop there. Even though He was a Son, he learned obedience through the things he suffered, and it qualified Him to become the author of eternal salvation. Because of His willful humility to the will of God, he was exalted with a name above every other name ever known to humanity.

If you are reading this and still feeling injured and hurt by the actions of a sister or brother in ministry, ask yourself this question. What is God qualifying me to be beyond this emotional injury that won't seem to let me go on with God's purpose for me within the church where He planted me? If God planted me here, He did it so I could grow, blossom, mature, and bear fruit. Growing up as a farmer, I learned that a plant cannot endure continual transplanting. The plant may live, but its growth will be severely slowed down, and it may never bear fruit.

The spiritual principle of growth is the same as the natural. A saint that continues to move from one congregation to another will stunt their growth, and they may never mature and bear fruit. In a contemporary society of unlimited choices, this may sound very wrong to suggest that someone should stand still to see the salvation of the

Lord or wait and be still and know that He is God. But in scriptural reality, **responsibility dropping, and church hopping** are not how Christ taught believers to handle offenses and conflicts (Matt 18:15-20).

> Believers are to consider themselves dead to sin: a dead person cannot feel anything (hurt).

Saints are to arm themselves with the mind of Christ so that, like Jesus, our thoughts will be conducive to embracing the benefits of suffering and maintaining coherence in Christ's body. Remember, the body of Christ is one body with many members. Often, the response to hurt is treating Christianity as if it is many bodies for the one hurt member to choose as an alternative option. Locating in another fellowship does not suggest that someone should remain in a toxic situation where authoritarianism, dogmatism, and various schisms dominate the fellowship environment. But the principle of the scripture is to exhaust all means of reconciliation before giving up. An offender is given three tries before being labeled ex-communicated. The approach is with the understanding that three in scripture may represent completion. In other words, the Holy Spirit may encourage the offended to try ten times (if they feel the person is coming around but is still reluctant to admit wrong), which would symbolize ten.

Because of the joy set before Him, Jesus endured the cross despite despising the shame. Yes, he died, but the death was not permanent, nor was it possible for death to hold a Holy one. The same is true for all members of the body of Christ. He declared himself to be the truth. I coined an expression that continues to help me when I feel hurt and wronged: *Time and Truth go Hand and Hand.* Truth is invincible against a permanent death. It can be abused, crucified, and buried. But in time, the truth will resurrect because lies have an expiration date. However, Truth is invincible against permanent death when it comes to death.

How hurt is processed in the mind can lead to persistent bondage to hurt, or the utilization of the prescribed meditation medication can lead to freedom from the unrelenting pain of feeling hurt by someone. Letting the mind of Christ be your mind is a conscious decision that one makes. A person can let the mind of Christ be their approach to being hurt in the body of Christ or not. But what a blessing it is to follow the example of Christ. Those who suffer in the flesh have ceased from sin (1 Pe.4:1). Those who suffer through it do it, knowing that the trying of their faith offers positive outcomes. So, believers can consider themselves dead to sin (Rom. 6:11) because a dead person cannot feel anything, including hurt feelings and emotions.

ARRESTING THE CRIMINAL MIND

Scripture sees the mind that is against the spirit as a criminal mind. Thoughts that are contrary to the will of God must be arrested and brought captive to comply with the will of God. For this, the Spirit of God provides for us weapons of warfare (2 Cor. 10:4-6). Our thoughts are considered carnal and criminal when they make suffering in the Lord's service a thing to be rejected and a reason to criticize and ostracize the Lord's church.

No matter the hurt, our hope in the resurrection power of the Holy Spirit is always available for our speedy recovery. Like Apostle Paul, our physical bodies may be left with an agitating thorn in the flesh (2 Cor. 12:7). Still, our cognitive response should not be a longing to exploit our hurts or become stuck with a feeling of spiritual paralysis. Scripture presents Christ's suffering in the flesh as the model for our suffering in the spiritual arena, the cure for avoiding having a lingering feeling of being wronged, and the cure for sin, not a curse on the saints. Those who suffer in their flesh have ceased from sin, including the desire to retaliate in the flesh (with a carnal mind).

Every thought that is not thinking like Christ should be brought captive to the will and knowledge of God. Believers must arrest all thoughts that rebel against the will of God by longing to exploit hurts that, if unchecked, will undermine the blessings and benefits of suffering for the glory of God. Christ, our example, even though He was a Son, He learned obedience by the things that he suffered. It is spiritually criminal to long to be treated better than Christ when we are hurt in Christian service. This criminal mind must be arrested and brought in line with the will of God.

Our hurts do not deserve to take complete control of our minds, as if our hurts deserve more attention and stroking than our faith in Jesus. When our thoughts tell us that something is wrong with the church and the church is the source of our injuries, the hurt believer must make a *citizen of heaven arrest.* We are citizens of heaven where we look for our savior's return (Phil. 3:20). So, when thoughts become criminal, they must be arrested!

If necessary, read your thoughts their rights. Your thoughts have the right to comply with the mind of Christ and the word of forgiveness because anything you say to the contrary will work out against you. God has already appointed a lawyer for you. His name is Jesus, and he is already in the presence of God making intercessions for you (Rom. 8:34). So, on the contrary, whatever you suffer for divine consequences is accompanied by a divine provision that enables you to bear it. Our Lord's grace is available in abundance so that you can bear the unbearable to the glory of God (2 Cor. 12:9). Our faith in Jesus is how we gain access to this necessary favor of God (Rom. 5:1) that makes all our hurts bearable and not a matter of incriminating the church that God purchased with His own blood (Acts 20:28).

VENGEANCE, GOD'S PREROGATIVE

Vengeance is Mine, and recompense; Their foot shall slip in due time; For the day of their calamity is at hand, And the things to come hasten upon them. For the LORD will judge His people And have compassion on His servants, When He sees that their power is gone, And there is no one remaining, bond or free. Deut 32:35-36

The Spirit of the Lord GOD is upon Me, Because the LORD has anointed Me To preach good tidings to the poor; He has sent Me to heal the brokenhearted, To proclaim liberty to the captives, And the opening of the prison to those who are bound; To proclaim the acceptable year of the LORD, And the day of vengeance of our God; To comfort all who

74

mourn, To console those who mourn in Zion, To give them beauty for ashes, The oil of joy for mourning, The garment of praise for the spirit of heaviness; That they may be called trees of righteousness, The planting of the LORD, that He may be glorified. Isa 61:1-3

As a disciple of Christ —called to take up my cross and follow Jesus, no matter how heavy it feels—I had to learn to resist the urge for vengeance One of the most profound lessons I've learned as a disciple no matter how heavy it feels—is to resist the urge for vengeance, no matter how deeply I've been hurt. When grief brought me to my lowest point, I suffered deeply as those close to me tried to make sense of my tragedy.

To say I was wounded would be an understatement. What made it even more painful was realizing that the hurtful words and actions came from people who knew me well—people I never expected would doubt my character or intentions. Well-meaning friends sometimes say things that unintentionally wound us, in their attempts to provide comfort. But there are also times when the fear of the unknown leads them to conclusions that fit the faith positions they already hold.

When someone's tragedy challenges another's beliefs, it can provoke accusations and blame. Even as I mourned the loss of a loved one to an aggressive cancer, I was told that my faith wasn't strong enough to prevent the tragedy. Later, when my journey through grief didn't match their expectations of how long or how deeply I should mourn, I was accused of being unfaithful or not loving enough.

Others' inability to find spiritual meaning in my suffering, combined with a lack of understanding about grief, led to many hurtful words and actions directed at me. Through this experience, I learned that the pain and loss of others often stir up fear and discomfort in those around them. This fear can cause even well-intentioned people to act in ways that are unintentionally hurtful.

Ultimately, I have come to understand that forgiveness and compassion are essential—not just for others, but for myself. Choosing not to retaliate, even when deeply wounded, is a powerful act of faith and discipleship.

I have since learned that when it comes to the loss and pain of others, it tends to cause fear and unsettlement in others close to the family. With my severely bruised spirit, it would have been easy for bitterness to turn into hurt and anger. Their actions felt like a personal attack—an attempt to destroy my character. I cried so much one night over being betrayed by those I trusted that I cried eventually myself to sleep. My heart ached so intensely that it felt like it was going to explode!

During that time, I wondered what to do and replayed the harsh judgmental words and attitudes while my heart was already broken. I questioned everything. Should I remain in ministry? Should I quit? I remember thinking that it was the best time to leave the ministry because everyone around me would understand my exit. Now I know that these thoughts were tempting me to sin against the calling and charge I received from the Holy Spirit: "Preach my word, I mean you, Preach my word!

I had seen God do so many amazing things yet look at what was happening to me! I saw no full recovery or forgiveness for those saying and doing hurtful things to me. The Lord spoke to me. I do not remember the time or place, but I remember the vivid warning that I received from the Lord. The Lord spoke these words to me: *"If you ever get bitter, I can never use you."*

It was that experience and similar ones that made me vow not ever to allow being hurt by others to hinder or control any aspect of my life or cause bitterness to contaminate my soul. The word bitter carries the connotation of poison. Bitterness is like poison to the soul of the one suffering the distasteful hurt that is real. Although I was spiritually numb with no desire to do for God, I never lost the desire to be used by God as His instrument. In retrospect, I understand the warning also to be words of hope. God loves me enough to warn me against the toxicity inherent in bitterness.

> The Lord said to me, "If you ever get bitter, I can never use you!"

Much later, I realized that when I had no desire to pray or talk to God, God still had plans to use me; His plan for me could've been hindered by my becoming bitter toward those who were causing me to hurt. Again, I will reiterate, they could have hurt me out of their fear of my unknown. Another possibility could have been interpreting my pain through the filters of a reformation that falls far short of the biblical teaching related to faith, prayer, death, healing, etc. Few things will have a Christian questioning their theological position, like an untimely death that does not make sense. Regardless of the reason, the pain and hurt that it cost me was real.

Grief is a natural part of life that is only understandable in the context of each situation. Those trying to use their personal experiences, beliefs, or theologies to explain or offer emphatic biblical reasons for pain and suffering are s treading on shaky spiritual ground. Losing a mother is unlike losing a child. Losing a child is unlike losing a brother, and losing a father is unlike losing a husband. Every relationship is unique. So no one can honestly say to a grieving person, "I know what you are going through." Though we all know what it means to grieve, every individual's grief is unique. While it might be possible to have sympathy for a person, having total empathy for another's experience may not be possible. This inability to be completely empathetic may cause us to jump to inaccurate conclusions regarding others. Jesus cautions His followers to avoid attempting to explain the root cause of others' pains or misfortune.

Now as Jesus passed by, He saw a man who was blind from birth. And His disciples asked Him, saying, "Rabbi, who sinned, this man or his parents, that he was born blind?" Jesus answered, "Neither this man nor his parents sinned, but that the works of God should be revealed in him. Jn 9:1-3

There were present at that season some who told Him about the Galileans whose blood Pilate had mingled with their sacrifices. And Jesus answered and said to them, "Do you suppose that these Galileans were worse sinners than all other Galileans, because they suffered such things? I tell you, no; but unless you repent you will all likewise perish. Or those eighteen on whom the tower in Siloam fell and killed them, do you think that they were worse sinners than all other men who dwelt in Jerusalem? I tell you, no; but unless you repent you will all likewise perish. Lk 13:1-5

Those who try to explain the tragedy of others in various ways that objectify the experience of others must consider their subjective biases to the same kinds of happenings. Understanding this truth should help hurt people from becoming bitter or attempting to retaliate against those who hurt them. Reaping is a natural part of sowing. Those who sow judgmental seeds will eventually grow and reap the harvest of judging, misjudging, and-or prejudging the root cause of the suffering of others. Likewise, to retaliate due to being hurt by the actions of others only complicates the matter for the one suffering. I often tell people, "Only sow what you want to grow." If you do not want to grow it, don't sow it." Sufferers must avoid becoming bitter about their experience, and instead allow God to handle any vengeance that is in order. Ironically, God said vengeance is mine. When God finally comes to get His vengeance, first, He steps into human flesh and allows Himself to endure all the feelings of

> Reaping is a natural part of sowing. Only sow what you want to grow.

our infirmities (Heb. 4:15). Then He becomes a vicarious sufferer who takes all the variations of sin on Himself.

For when we were still without strength, in due time Christ died for the ungodly... But God demonstrates His own love toward us, in that while we were still sinners, Christ died for us. **Rom 5:6-8**

For He made Him who knew no sin to be sin for us, that we might become the righteousness of God in Him. ***2 Cor 5:21***

He saw that there was no man, And wondered that there was no intercessor; Therefore His own arm brought salvation for Him; And His own righteousness, it sustained Him. **Isa 59:16**

All this is from God, who reconciled us to himself through Christ and gave us the ministry of reconciliation: that God was reconciling the world to himself in Christ, not counting people's sins against them. And he has committed to us the message of reconciliation. 2 Cor 5:18-19

God's mode of retaliation was for His *own* power to bring about salvation for the entire world: by becoming a human to save His weak enemies and create a pathway for reconciliation. He uses the hurt of others to be the healing for the ones who hurt Him. Oh, the power and paradox in the wisdom of God! When getting vengeance is left up to God, victory is always possible. He turns our hurt into something that can bring reconciliation with those who cause the hurt. Jesus models this for His followers.

But I say unto you, Love your enemies, bless them that curse you, do good to them that hate you, and pray for them which despitefully use you, and persecute you; Matt 5:44

Therefore, if anyone is in Christ, he is a new creation; old things have passed away; behold, all things have become new. Now all things are of God, who has reconciled us to Himself through Jesus Christ, and has given us the ministry of reconciliation, that is, that God was in Christ reconciling the world to Himself, not imputing their trespasses to them, and has committed to us the word of reconciliation. 2 Cor 5:17-19

There are times when reconciliation is *not possible*, but when and where it is possible, it is always powerful enough to bring healing to all parties involved.

Surely He has borne our griefs And carried our sorrows; Yet we esteemed Him stricken, Smitten by God, and afflicted. But He was wounded for our transgressions, He was bruised for our iniquities; The chastisement for our peace was upon Him, And by His stripes we are healed. All we like sheep have gone astray; We have turned, everyone, to his own way; And the LORD has laid on Him the iniquity of us all. Isa 53:4-6

PERMANENT HEALING: LOVING TO THE END

PRESCRIPTION 7 - MEDITATION MEDICATION:
MEDICINE FROM HEAVEN FOR HEALING ON EARTH

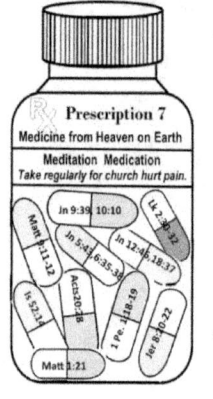

Just as many were astonished at you, So His visage was marred more than any man, And His form more than the sons of men; Isa 52:14

Therefore take heed to yourselves and to all the flock, among which the Holy Spirit has made you overseers, to shepherd the church of God which He purchased with His own blood. Acts 20:28

knowing that you were not redeemed with corruptible things, like silver or gold, from your aimless conduct received by tradition from your fathers, but with the precious blood of Christ, as of a lamb without blemish and without spot. 1 Ptr 1:18-19.

The harvest is past, the summer is ended, and we are not saved. For the hurt of the daughter of my people am I hurt; I am black; astonishment hath taken hold on me. Is there no balm in Gilead; is there no physician there? Why then is not the health of the daughter of my people recovered? Jer 8:20-22

And when the Pharisees saw it, they said to His disciples, "Why does your teacher eat with tax collectors and sinners?" When Jesus heard that, He said to them, "Those who are well have no need of a physician, but those who are sick. Several places in John's gospel Jesus mentions why he came into the world. Matt 9:11-12

And Jesus said to them, "I am the bread of life. He who comes to Me shall never hunger, and he who believes in Me shall never thirst. But I said to you that you have seen Me and yet do not believe. All that the Father gives Me will come to Me, and the one who comes to Me I will by no means cast out. For I have come down from heaven, not to do My own will, but the will of Him who sent Me. Jn 6:35-38

I have come *in My Father's name, and you do not receive Me; if another comes in his own name, him you will receive.* Jn 5:43

And Jesus said, "For judgment **I have come** *into this world, that those who do not see may see, and that those who see may be made blind."* Jn 9:39

The thief does not come except to steal, and to kill, and to destroy. **I have come** *that they may have life, and that they may have it more abundantly.* Jn 10:10

I have come as a light into the world, that whoever believes in Me should not abide in darkness Jn 12:46.

Pilate therefore said to Him, "Are You a king then?" Jesus answered, "You say rightly that I am a king. For this cause I was born, and for this cause **I have come** *into the world, that I should bear witness to the truth. Everyone who is of the truth hears My voice.* Jn 18:37

Simeon a devout man that was waiting for the consolation of Israel, takes the baby Jesus in His arms and blesses God with **the** *words: For my eyes have seen Your salvation Which You have prepared before the face of all peoples, A light to bring revelation to the Gentiles, And the glory of Your people Israel.* Lk 2:30-32

And she will bring forth a Son, and you shall call His name JESUS, for He will save His people from their sins. Matt 1:21

WHERE'S THE MEDICINE FOR MY HURTING SOUL?

Jesus was medicine from heaven sent to bring a permanent cure for sin. He came to earth on a recovery mission. God's blood ran through His veins, the antidote for the aggressive cancerous disease of sin. God purchased the church with His blood that was shed through the pores of the body of Jesus: from the crown of thorns crushed into His temple, and the nails driven through His feet and hands to fasten Him to the cross. The skin covering His body from head to toe would have been torn into shreds with wounds, cuts, and bruises. So much so that Isaiah stated prophetically that it was marred more than any other human. However, His precious sinless blood was the medicine to cure the terminal disease of sin.

The first two chapters of Genesis contain a snapshot of God's will for humanity. But from Genesis three forward, the Father's will was severely challenged by the knowledge of evil. Jesus came in His Father's name because His will is not done on earth like in Heaven. There is no hurt in Heaven. Evil, and darkness, had lingered on the planet, causing death and destruction (Jn 1:1-2, 3:16-18). John's gospel tells us His Father's will includes executing judgment so that the blind will have a chance to see. But those who see but ignore the light may be a victim of their choice. And will be permanently spiritually blind (Jn 9).

84

Jesus comes to bring the truth to light that will dispel the darkness that's caused by those whose deeds are evil (Jn 1:5, 3:19). He comes first to His own, the Jews who were chosen to be God's light in the world that led people back to God (1:11). Jesus would represent Israel to do what they did not do: be a light to the Gentiles showing them the way back to God, the creator of all (Isa 49:6, Lk 2:30-32). They were to be a light to the Gentiles; instead, they were a primary cause of spiritual darkness. Also, He has come into the world to combat the threefold agenda of the thief, to steal, kill, and destroy, by offering a chance for all to enjoy life the way God intended it to be from the beginning (Jn 10:10).

Unfortunately, at the time of Jesus, the Jews, with their leadership, which God had chosen to represent Him and be a light to the nations, were the primary enforcers of the lies that plunged the world into spiritual darkness. God chose Israel to fulfill His will and be a light to the nations that would guide them back to Him, their creator. But as a nation, they failed to do God's will. God sent His son into the world to represent them and to bring about God's purpose to bless all people through Abraham (Gen.12:1-4). Jesus was keenly aware of who He was, why He was on earth, what the rejection of Him meant for the Jewish nation, and what it meant for the entire world. As the time drew near for Him to reach the climax of the Father's will and why He had come to earth, he reflected on what was about to occur.

Prescription 8 - Meditation Medication: *Correctly Diagnose the Hurt*

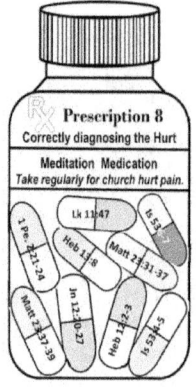

O Jerusalem, Jerusalem, thou that killest the prophets, and stonest them which are sent unto thee, how often would I have gathered thy children together, even as a hen gathereth her chickens under her wings, and ye would not! Behold, your house is left unto you desolate. For I say unto you, Ye shall not see me henceforth, till ye shall say, Blessed is he that cometh in the name of the Lord. Matt 23:37-39

And there were certain Greeks among them that came up to worship at the feast: The same came therefore to Philip, which was of Bethsaida of Galilee, and desired him, saying, Sir, we would see Jesus. Philip cometh and telleth Andrew: and again Andrew and Philip tell Jesus. And Jesus answered them, saying, The hour is come, that the Son of man should be glorified. Verily, verily, I say unto you, Except a corn of wheat fall into the ground and die, it abideth alone: but if it die, it bringeth forth much fruit. He that loveth his life shall lose it; and he that hateth his life in this world shall keep it unto life eternal. If any man serve me, let him follow me; and where I am, there shall also my servant be: if any man serve me, him will my Father honour. Now is my soul troubled; and what shall I say? Father, save me from this hour: but for this cause came I unto this hour. Jn 12:20-27

looking unto Jesus, the author and finisher of our faith, who for the joy that was set before Him endured the cross, despising the shame, and has sat down at the right hand of the throne of God. ³ For consider Him who endured such hostility from sinners against Himself, lest you become weary and discouraged in your souls. Heb 12:2-3

86

Surely He has borne our griefs And carried our sorrows; Yet we esteemed Him stricken, Smitten by God, and afflicted. ⁵ But He was wounded for our transgressions, He was bruised for our iniquities; The chastisement for our peace was upon Him, And by His stripes we are healed. Isa 53:4-**5**

For even hereunto were ye called: because Christ also suffered for us, leaving us an example, that ye should follow his steps: Who did no sin, neither was guile found in his mouth: Who, when he was reviled, reviled not again; when he suffered, he threatened not; but committed himself to him that judgeth righteously: Who his own self bare our sins in his own body on the tree, that we, being dead to sins, should live unto righteousness: by whose stripes ye were healed. 1 Ptr 2:21-24

A proper diagnosis for any disease is critical for knowing what medicine to prescribe. The disease of sin is no exception. Once prophets like Isaiah revealed that the actual cause of continual sickness and hurting souls was rooted in sin, God gave a prognosis for recovery: a vicarious suffering servant to become the general cure for the root cause of pain, including church hurt. On so many recovery levels, Jesus answered the questions enacted by Jeremiah centuries earlier. Is there no medicine? If there is, then why are the daughters of my people still sick?

Of course, the answer is that they refuse to swallow and digest the treatment written in their covenant relationship document: inherent in the Pentateuch. God repeatedly sent prophets to Israel with a message of healing. The healing message was ignored. Repeatedly, they refused the diagnoses and prognoses. As Jesus states in different ways, they killed the messengers who had the medicine for their hurt (Matt

23:31-37 Lk 11:47). What Isaiah saw as a coming future cure for sin, the cancer of the soul (Is. 53), Peter sees as being accomplished in the wounds, bruises and chastisements of Jesus who took our sins on himself (1 Ptr 2:24). This cure for all our hurts has no expiration date:

Jesus Christ is the same yesterday, today, and forever. **Heb 13:8**.

To suggest that the word of God is still the cure for our hurts, including church hurt, may sound too simple for what appears to be a complicated issue in our complex church environment. We indeed live in a challenging church culture where issues of conflict vary. However, the word of God is still God's medication for all that ails us, regardless of the world in which we live.

Jesus endured the cross because of the joy before Him. There is no indication that the joy He saw before Him ended at the close of the first century. Yes, we have complicated our world with unimaginable complexities, but Jesus Christ is the same as He has always been the lamb of God who takes away the world's sins. As Pentecostals joyfully sing: The blood still works, and the blood never loses its power! Glory to God.

Jesus was not looking forward to the painful ordeal that awaited Him, but having our sins beat into His innocent body so he could carry them to the grave was the climax of His purpose for being on earth. His wounds, stripes, and chastisement provide healing for all believers, including the recovery from the causes of church hurt. Medicine is available for all the hurts we encounter as we walk with the

Lord. However, medication is not good on the shelf, and physicians are

PRESCRIPTION 9 - MEDITATION MEDICATION: LOVE THE TRUTH OF GOD'S WORD.

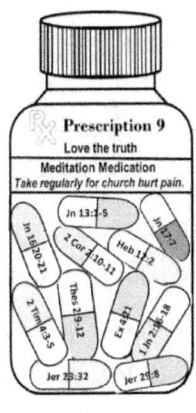

Behold, I am against those who prophesy false dreams," says the LORD, "and tell them, and cause My people to err by their lies and by their recklessness. Yet I did not send them or command them; therefore, they shall not profit this people at all," says the LORD. Jer 23:32

For thus says the LORD of hosts, the God of Israel: Do not let your prophets and your diviners who are in your midst deceive you, nor listen to your dreams which you cause to be dreamed. Jer 29:8

For the time will come when they will not endure sound doctrine, but according to their own desires, because they have itching ears, they will heap up for themselves teachers; and they will turn their ears away from the truth, and be turned aside to fables. But you be watchful in all things, endure afflictions, do the work of an evangelist, fulfill your ministry. 2 Tim 4:3-5 [3]

The coming of the lawless one is according to the working of Satan, with all power, signs, and lying wonders, and with all unrighteous deception among those who perish, because they did not receive the love of the truth, that they might be saved. And for this reason God will send them strong delusion, that they should believe the lie, that they all may be condemned who did not believe the truth but had pleasure in unrighteousness. 2 Thess 2:9-12

And the LORD said unto Moses, when thou goest to return into Egypt, see that thou do all those wonders before Pharaoh, which I have put in thine hand: but I will harden his heart, that he shall not let the people go. Ex 4:21

Loving the truth of God's word is a spiritual immune system builder. As in the time of Jeremiah, medicine was available, but the people refused to take it. The medication was the word of God that Jeremiah and other prophets before him kept providing for the community: but the community kept rejecting it for their homegrown remedies. The homegrown remedies were false prophets telling them what they wanted to hear. Ultimately, it caused so many deaths because sin is still a terminal disease that leads to death. The twenty first century church must not make the same mistake, for this is the last hour before the Lord's return (1 Jn 2:18).

Two thousand years ago, the church was in the *last hour*. So, it would not be presumptuous to think that we could now be in the last few minutes of the last hour. Those who read these soul-healing scriptures and continue to persist in church hurt should consider deeply the word of scripture.

For all that is in the world--the lust of the flesh, the lust of the eyes, and the pride of life—is not of the Father but is of the world. And the world is passing away, and the lust of it; but he who does the will of God abides forever. Little children, it is the last hour; and as you have heard that the Antichrist is coming, even now many antichrists have come, by which we know that it is the last hour. 1 Jn 2:16-18

BIRTH PAINS FOR SPIRITUAL GAIN

Most assuredly, I say to you that you will weep and lament, but the world will rejoice; and you will be sorrowful, but your sorrow will be turned into joy. [21] A woman, when she is in labor, has sorrow because her hour has come; but as soon as she has given birth to the child, she no longer remembers the anguish, for joy that a human being has been born into the world. Therefore you now have sorrow; but I will see you again and your heart will rejoice, and your joy no one will take from you. Jn 16:20-22

> *Looking unto Jesus, the author and finisher of our faith, who for the joy that was set before Him endured the cross, despising the shame, and has sat down at the right hand of the throne of God.* Heb 12:2

> *Now before the feast of the Passover, when Jesus knew that His hour had come that He should depart from this world to the Father, having loved His own who were in the world, He loved them to the end. And supper being ended, the devil having already put it into the heart of Judas Iscariot, Simon's son, to betray Him, Jesus, knowing that the Father had given all things into His hands, and that He had come from God and was going to God, rose from supper and laid aside His garments, took a towel and girded Himself. After that, He poured water into a basin and began to wash the disciples' feet, and to wipe them with the towel with which He was girded.* **Jn 13:1-5**

Giving birth to the church was a painful experience for our Lord and Savior, Jesus Christ, and those he drew close to him. Jesus compared the experience to that of a woman giving birth. The birth pains intensify, and when the baby comes, the pains subside because the focus is on the new life. Jesus was deeply hurt giving birth to the church, but because of the joy set before him, He willfully endured it all.

91

ENDLESS LOVE: THE CHURCH HURT CURE

PRESCRIPTION 10: MEDITATION MEDICATION: APPLYING LOVE THAT HEALS WHILE IT HURTS.

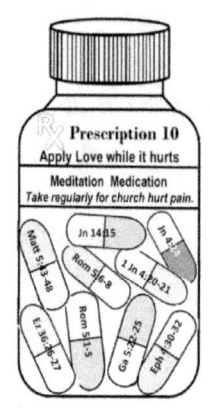

A new heart also will I give you, and a new spirit will I put within you: and I will take away the stony heart out of your flesh, and I will give you an heart of flesh. [27] And I will put my spirit within you, and cause you to walk in my statutes, and ye shall keep my judgments, and do them. Ezk36:26-27 (11:19)

Therefore, having been justified by faith, we have peace with God through our Lord Jesus Christ, [2] through whom also we have access by faith into this grace in which we stand, and rejoice in hope of the glory of God. And not only that, but we also glory in tribulations, knowing that tribulation produces perseverance; and perseverance, character; and character, hope. Now hope does not disappoint, because the love of God has been poured out in our hearts by the Holy Spirit who was given to us. Rom 5:1-5

But the fruit of the Spirit is love, joy, peace, longsuffering, kindness, goodness, faithfulness, gentleness, self-control. Against such there is no law. And those who are Christ's have crucified the flesh with its passions and desires. [2]If we live in the Spirit, let us also walk in the Spirit. Gal 5:22-25

And do not grieve the Holy Spirit of God, by whom you were sealed for the day of redemption. Let all bitterness, wrath, anger, clamor, and evil speaking be put away from you, with all malice. And be kind to one another, tenderhearted, forgiving one another, just as God in Christ forgave you. Eph 4:30-32

You have heard that it was said, 'You shall love your neighbor and hate your enemy.' But I say to you, love your enemies, bless those who curse you, do good to those who hate you, and pray for those who spitefully use you and persecute you, that you may be sons of your Father in heaven; for He makes His sun rise on the evil and on the good, and sends rain on the just and on the unjust. For if you love those who love you, what reward have you? Do not even the tax collectors do the same? And if you greet your brethren only, what do you do more than others? Do not even the tax collectors do so? Therefore you shall be perfect, just as your Father in heaven is perfect. Matt 5:43-48

For when we were still without strength, in due time Christ died for the ungodly. For scarcely for a righteous man will one die; yet perhaps for a good man someone would even dare to die. But God demonstrates His own love toward us, in that while we were still sinners, Christ died for us. Rom 5:6-8

If you love Me, keep My commandments. Jn 14:15

If someone says, "I love God," and hates his brother, he is a liar; for he who does not love his brother whom he has seen, how can he love God whom he has not seen? [21] And this commandment we have from Him: that he who loves God must love his brother also. 1 Jn 4:20-21

God is Spirit, and those who worship Him must worship in spirit and truth. Jn 4:24

Scripture contains healing ingredients for those who obey and meditate on them. *"Love your enemies, bless those who curse you, do good to those who hate you, and pray for those who spitefully use you and persecute you"* These commandments are not optional duties for Spirit-filled followers of Jesus. To think or behave differently and still profess to be Jesus' disciple is like saying "dry water." Keeping Jesus's commands by expressing God's love toward others validates our love *for* God. Loving our enemies and praying for our persecutors demonstrates love that requires forgiveness. In essence, those who have a love *for* God (vertical) will demonstrate it with the love *of* God (horizontal), even toward enemies. Jesus speaks this command in the context of praying for those who are sources of pain and hurt. Water can never be dry, and love for God is impossible without a passion for the people who God loves. God so loves the world that he gave the world the best heaven had to offer: Jesus, the word made flesh (Jn 3:16). We must model the love Jesus demonstrated before the world so that the world will associate the Church with Jesus. God so loved the world that he gave the world Jesus. Disciples are to continue to provide the world with Jesus by loving each other the way Jesus loved us: without restrictions. Jesus loved the world to His death, and with His Spirit comes the power to die to self so others can see the life of Jesus revealed through our actions.

Seeing suffering as an intricate part of ministry requires new thinking that is only possible for those with a new heart and spirit (Eze. 35). The love of God is poured out into the heart (soul) by the Holy Spirit (Rom. 5:5). When the Holy Spirit comes to live within an individual, He brings with him the love of God required to obey the will of God. The indwelling Holy Spirit is how radical love for one's enemy is possible. The fruit of the Spirit is love, joy, peace, forbearance, kindness, goodness, faithfulness, gentleness, and self-control are all facets of love (Gal. 5:22-23) (compare *Gal 5:22-23* with *1 Cor 13:4-8,* and *Jn 15:L9-17)*. Therefore, loving one's enemies is only possible with a new heart and spirit. So, to think and behave correctly toward suffering and hurt in ministry, one must have the Holy Spirit living within. In this case, God's will is that love be without hesitation or restrictions, even

> The Word May taste *Bitter* while making you *Better.*

for those who hurt us. This love empowers the Spirit-filled believer to embrace affliction in ministry for the benefits it brings including gaining patience from tribulation and the trying of our faith that generates patience). Obeying this command is a sign of spiritual maturity. It aligns God's servant with our heavenly Father, who sends His rain on the just and the unjust (Matt 5:45). I encourage everyone suffering from any form of church hurt to take this medication before reacting in unscriptural ways. Apply this *love that heals while it hurts.* This medicine from the word of God does not always taste good. And suffer from church hurt, that continues to linger in your heart, this is the best medication to take. Those who medicate themselves with this meditation day and night *will be well on their way to living a "church-hurt-free"* life.

In everything give thanks: for this is the will of God in Christ Jesus concerning you. 1 Thess 5:18

Love Demonstration – A Case Study

Now before the feast of the Passover, when Jesus knew that His hour had come that He should depart from this world to the Father, having loved His own who were in the world, He loved them to the end. ² And supper being ended, the devil having already put it into the heart of Judas Iscariot, Simon's son, to betray Him Jn 13:1-2

The church hurt cure begins with modeling every thought and behavior after the love demonstrated by Jesus who loved His disciples to the end. This case study for the cure for church hurt is unpacked in John chapters thirteen through seventeen. In this narrative, Jesus spends His final hours with future church leaders. only hours away from suffering and dying a horrific sacrificial death, He is in an intimate setting with them, he holds a final conversation before His arrest. So this teaching must last.

The synoptic gospels (Matthew, Mark, and Luk) detail the side conversations leading up to this teaching moment in time. That night they had a Passover meal that Jesus transformed into a new covenant-making meal once supper had ended. During the new covenant-making ritual, Jesus fed their spirits with a radical departure from how they understood love and how it should be applied and expressed.

He was holding a leadership seminar with those who would have to model his ministry after He departs from the world: In this final meeting before His arrest, He discussed vital information about what it would take for His disciples to be like Him without His physical presence. **Since the Holy Spirit inspired the gospel writings years after the**

events occurred, John chapters 13 through 17 can be seen as the Holy Spirit's notes from that seminar. Köstenberger notes, "While the first part of John's Gospel shows Jesus' rejection by Israel, the remainder focuses on Jesus' preparation of his new covenant community to continue his mission following his crucifixion and resurrection."[1] Although Jesus was preparing them for greatness that only His approach to love could accomplish, they were busy seeking the greatness defined by the culture. Their thinking was far from the thoughts of Jesus.

WHAT THE TWELVE APOSTLES WERE THINKING

Pocketbook: Judas focused on filling his pocket with extra finances at the expense of Jesus and the other apostles: he betrayed Jesus for thirty pieces of silver. However, the same night Judas betrayed Jesus, the devil had already put it in his heart to sell out Jesus. Judas was waiting for the right opportunity to commit this wrong deed. The intention was not only in his thoughts. It was in his heart. Sin around us is a matter of temptation, but once sin enters our hearts, it is a matter of condemnation. Jesus notes that what comes out of us defiles us, not what goes in us: because what comes out of us comes directly from the heart (Matt 15:10-19). So, when they gathered that night, Judas was already defiled (dirty) because of the evil intentions in his heart. Like a

---

[1] A. J. Köstenberger, "Mission" in *New Dictionary of Biblical Theology*, ed. T. Desmond Alexander and Brian S. Rosner, (Downers Grove, IL: InterVarsity Press, 2000), 667.

treasurer, he had the Apostle's purse. In the end, the pocketbook proves to be his undoing.

Then one of the twelve, called Judas Iscariot, went to the chief priests and said, "What are you willing to give me if I deliver Him to you?" And they counted out to him thirty pieces of silver. So from that time he sought opportunity to betray Him. Matt 26:14-16

Then Mary took a pound of very costly oil of spikenard, anointed the feet of Jesus, and wiped His feet with her hair. And the house was filled with the fragrance of the oil. Then one of His disciples, Judas Iscariot, Simon's son, who would betray Him, said, "Why was this fragrant oil not sold for three hundred denarii and given to the poor?" This he said, not that he cared for the poor, but because he was a thief, and had the money box; and he used to take what was put in it. Jn 12:3-6

But behold, the hand of My betrayer is with Me on the table. And truly the Son of Man goes as it has been determined, but woe to that man by whom He is betrayed!" Then they began to question among themselves, which of them it was who would do this thing. Lk 22:21-23

And supper being ended, the devil having already put it into the heart of Judas Iscariot, Simon's son, to betray Him Jn 13:2

Power: Having power was the desire of all twelve apostles. They were discussing who would be the greatest among them. James and John's mother helped them to ask Jesus for seats next to Him in His kingdom. The rest were upset with them for doing so. The scene indicates that they may have been upset because James and John did something they all wanted but they beat them to it.

98

And there was also a strife among them, which of them should be accounted the greatest. And he said unto them, The kings of the Gentiles exercise lordship over them; and they that exercise authority upon them are called benefactors. But ye shall not be so: but he that is greatest among you, let him be as the younger; and he that is chief, as he that doth serve.
Lk 22:24-26

Politics and Position: James and John, along with their mother lobbied Jesus for a chance to sit on His right and His left in His kingdom.

Then the mother of Zebedee's sons came to Him with her sons, kneeling down and asking something from Him. And He said to her, "What do you wish?" She said to Him, "Grant that these two sons of mine may sit, one on Your right hand and the other on the left, in Your kingdom." But Jesus answered and said, "You do not know what you ask. Are you able to drink the cup that I am about to drink, and be baptized with the baptism that I am baptized with?"... Matt 20:20-22

When Jesus was thinking of Love to the end, they were lusting for five love killers that continued to suck the life out of ministries: *purse, power, politics, position, and pride.* It is worth noting that this thinking and atmosphere among the future leaders saw the rise of Judas. Although Jesus knew Judas was plotting His betrayal, He did not expose him. Instead, Jesus loved him to the end as He did the rest of them.

When Jesus had said these things, He was troubled in spirit, and testified and said, "Most assuredly, I say to you, one of you will betray Me."... Now after the piece of bread, Satan entered him. Then Jesus said to him, "What you do, do quickly." But no one at the table knew for what reason He said this to him. For some thought, because Judas had the money box, that Jesus had said to him, "Buy those things we need for the feast," or that he should give something to the poor. Having received the piece of bread, he then went out immediately. And it was night. Jn 13:21, 27-30

Now His betrayer had given them a sign, saying, "Whomever I kiss, He is the One; seize Him." Immediately he went up to Jesus and said, "Greetings, Rabbi!" and kissed Him. But Jesus said to him, "Friend, why have you come?" Then they came and laid hands-on Jesus and took Him. Matt 26:48-50

And while he yet spake, behold a multitude, and he that was called Judas, one of the twelve, went before them, and drew near unto Jesus to kiss him. But Jesus said unto him, Judas, betrayest thou the Son of man with a kiss? Lk 22:47-48

I do not speak concerning all of you. I know whom I have chosen; but that the Scripture may be fulfilled, 'He who eats bread with Me has lifted up his heel against Me.' Jn 13:18

Judas deeply hurt the Lord in ministry, yet Jesus loved him *to the end*. When describing the actions of Judas, Jesus quoted from a Psalm that further reveals the depth of this love that enabled Jesus to keep loving the one who hurt Him.

Yea, mine own familiar friend, in whom I trusted, which did eat of my bread, hath lifted up his heel against me. Ps 41:9

For some of them thought, because Judas had the bag, that Jesus had said unto him, Buy those things that we have need of against the feast; or, that he should give something to the poor. Jn 13:29

The Lord trusted Judas so that the other disciples had no clue about what He was plotting to do. The prophecy of Zechariah points to some emotional hurt that Jesus, our Lord, received while carrying out the will of God.

Awake, O sword, against my shepherd, and against the man that is my fellow, saith the LORD of hosts: smite the shepherd, and the sheep shall be scattered: and I will turn mine hand upon the little ones. Zech 13:7

No servant is more significant than their master. The notion of church hurt must be seen for all its worth: the church work of filling up the afflictions left behind by our master (Col.1:24).

WHAT JESUS WAS THINKING

Jesus, knowing that the Father had given all things into His hands, and that He had come from God and was going to God, rose from supper and laid aside His garments, took a towel and girded Himself. After that, He poured water into a basin and began to wash the disciples' feet, and to wipe them with the towel with which He was girded. Jn 13:3-5

Jesus knew that the time of His departure was drawing close. He was thinking about what it would take for His disciples not to be destroyed by the killer P's —*purse, power, politics, position, and pride* (13:5). He was thinking about the kind of love that it would take for them to make it together (Jn13:34). He thought about how the fate of humanity rested on Him and those who would continue through the power of the Holy Spirit (Jn13:3). The Holy Spirit, the Spirit of Truth, would represent Him and comfort them leading them into all truth, after His departure to glory (Jn 16:13). He began to show them in a graphic way the love they must display for the world to associate them with Him (Jn 13:35). He begins with a lesson in humility to demonstrate what they must do for each other to stay humble and serve to combat the spirit of pride. With this and more of the same in mind, Jesus does something that refocuses their attention on helping each other versus striving against each other. He models every man for each other in opposition to every man for himself. Jesus got up from the table, poured water into a basin, and starts to wash His disciples' feet.

> *Then He came to Simon Peter. And Peter said to Him, "Lord, are You washing my feet?" Jesus answered and said to him, "What I am doing you do not understand now, but you will know after this." Peter said to Him, "You shall never wash my feet!" Jesus answered him, "If I do not wash you, you have no part with Me." Simon Peter said to Him, "Lord, not my feet only, but also my hands and my head!"* Jn 13:6-9

For Peter, what Jesus did was inconsistent with someone of His caliber, power, position, and authority. He viewed the Lord as too great to do such a task reserved for peasants. Simon Peter did not want the Lord to wash His feet. But the Lord makes it clear that he was modeling what it would take for them to represent Him in a world in dire need of His perspective on having power through being a servant to others. After Peter realizes that not allowing Jesus to wash his feet meant being separated from Him, Peter sought Jesus to wash his hands and his head: a complete bath. Peter is fully committed to Jesus. The expression, "his heart was in the right place," describes *Peter's attitude.*

> *Jesus said to him, "He who is bathed needs only to wash his feet, but is completely clean; and you are clean, but not all of you." For He knew who would betray Him; therefore He said, "You are not all clean." So when He had washed their feet, taken His garments, and sat down again, He said to them,* **"Do you know what I have done to you?** *You call me Teacher and Lord, and you say well, for so I am. 'If I then, your Lord and Teacher, have washed your feet, you also ought to wash one another's feet. For I have given you an example, that you should do as I have done to you. Most assuredly, I say to you, a servant is not greater than his master; nor is he who is sent greater than he who sent him.* Jn 13:10-16

At this point, Jesus reveals a more profound significance to washing their feet. Jesus' response indicates that Peter does not need a total cleansing, but there is one among them who does: the betrayer. Peter only had dirt on His feet, so He did not need a full bath. However, the one who would betray Him (Judas) was dirty all over, and cleaning him would require a full bath. The response of Jesus morphs from a natural meaning to a profoundly spiritual one. To clarify the spiritual significance of what He did, Jesus asked them if they knew what He had done to them.

What Jesus Did to them

Now there were set there six waterpots of stone, *according to the manner of purification of the Jews, containing twenty or thirty gallons apiece.* [7] *Jesus said to them, "Fill the waterpots with water." And they filled them up to the brim.* Jn 2:6-7 (NKJV)

And he turned to the woman, and said unto Simon, "Seest thou this woman? I entered into thine house, thou gavest me no water for my feet: but she hath washed my feet with tears and wiped them with the hairs of her head." Lk 7:44

The passages of scripture above help to explain the background for the attitudes about the washing of feet. Jesus did something that was customarily done, but certainly not by a rabbi or one who was a host for guests.

The backdrop for this scene is amazing. While they are discussing their agenda and lust for power, Jesus does something that is the ultimate expression of servanthood: he knelt and began to wash His disciples' feet. Palestine was a dry and dusty place. Since they either went barefoot or wore sandals, their feet would have been dusty and dirty. It was an act of hospitality, especially in well to do homes, to have servants wash guests' feet. Simon disrespected Jesus by inviting him to his home and neglecting a basic rule of hospitality: having water to wash his feet. But Jesus implies it was not a mistake, but a conscious decision to disrespect Him.

Some theologians suggest that the six waterpots Jesus turned to wine were originally intended for the Jewish custom of purification, possibly used for washing the guests' feet. Traditionally, performing this humble and often unpleasant task was reserved for servants, enslaved people, or those of the lowest social status. But during the gathering, Jesus interrupted the night's happenings to perform this menial chore. Everyone knew someone should have performed the task, but no one was willing to do it. Their focus was on *power* and gaining a *position in the* anticipated *kingdom*. They considered washing and drying dirty feet beneath them—a dirty job left for the least among them. By stepping forward to wash His disciples' feet, Jesus provided a powerful example of true service, showing that genuine leadership means embracing humility and being willing to serve others, even in the lowliest ways.

While telling us of Jesus doing the dirty job, John contrasted Peter and Judas. Several times he mentions the one who would betray Jesus. Yet Peter and Jesus do most of the talking. Peter would later sin by denying against Jesus. However, Judas's actions were even more severe, as he was actively plotting and preparing to betray Him

Unaware of future events, Peter dirties his reputation by adamantly insisting he would never deny Jesus. But Judas is dirty inside and out because Satan had already put it in his heart to betray Jesus. Earlier, Jesus had taught that it was not what goes into a person that defiles them but what comes out of them. What comes out of a person's mouth comes from their heart. Peter miscalculates what he is willing to do, but Judas is calculating what he would do.

In oscillating between the actions of Peter and Judas (chapter 13), John highlights the two significant types of sin that cause Jesus to love the world to His own sacrificial death.

But He was wounded for our transgressions, He was bruised for our iniquities; The chastisement for our peace was upon Him, And by His stripes we are healed. Isa53:5

Related to the idea of church hurt, there are two major categories of cancerous soul sins that the stripes of Jesus permanently cure. Both iniquity and transgression find atonement in the blood of Jesus. Iniquity—the first is the sin—is unintentional offenses or mistakes (faults or perversion) that are part of human DNA due to the sin of the first man Adam.

Therefore, just as through one man sin entered the world, and death through sin, and thus death spread to all men, because all sinned. Rom 5:12

And He has made from one blood every nation of men to dwell on all the face of the earth, and has determined their pre-appointed times and the boundaries of their dwellings… Acts 17:26

Importantly, all sacrifices in the Mosaic law were for unintentional sins or mistakes by an individual or the community. As portrayed in Leviticus and Numbers.

The LORD said to Moses, "Say to the Israelites: When anyone sins unintentionally and does what is forbidden in any of the LORD's commands— " If the anointed priest sins, bringing guilt on the people, he must bring to the LORD a young bull without defect as a sin offering for the sin he has committed. **Lev 4:1-3**

If the whole Israelite community sins unintentionally and does what is forbidden in any of the LORD's commands, even though the community is unaware of the matter, when they realize their guilt and the sin they committed becomes known, the assembly must bring a young bull as a sin offering and present it before the tent of meeting. **Lev 4:13-14**

Now if you as a community **unintentionally** *fail to keep any of these commands the LORD gave Moses— any of the LORD's commands to you through him, from the day the LORD gave them and continuing through the generations to come— and if this is done* **unintentionally** *without the community being aware of it, then the whole community is to offer a young bull for a burnt offering as an aroma pleasing to the LORD, along with its prescribed grain offering and drink offering, and a male goat for a sin offering. The priest is to make atonement for the whole Israelite community, and they will be forgiven,* **for it was not intentional** *and they have presented to the LORD for their wrong a food offering and a sin offering.* Num 15:22-25

In the law, there was no sacrifice for willful rebellion or intentional sin. The penalty for transgression, willful sins, and rebellion was death— usually by stoning or hanging.

For everyone that curseth his father or his mother shall be surely put to death: he hath **cursed his father or his mother; his blood shall be upon him.** Lev 20:9

And the man that committeth adultery with another man's wife, even he that committeth adultery with his neighbour's wife, the adulterer and the adulteress shall surely be put to **death.** Lev 20:10

And if a man have committed a sin worthy of death, and he be to be put to death, and thou hang him on a tree: His body shall not remain all night upon the tree, but thou shalt in any wise bury him that day; (for

107

he that is hanged is accursed of God;) that thy land be not defiled, which the LORD thy God giveth thee for an inheritance. Deut 21:22-23

Christ has redeemed us from the curse of the law, having become a curse for us (for it is written, "Cursed is everyone who hangs on a tree") Gal 3:13

Curing one's parents or committing adultery are intentional acts and when the sin was intentional in Israel, the penalty was death:

For if we sin willfully after that we have received the knowledge of the truth, there remaineth no more sacrifice for sins Heb 10:26

Jesus is the only sacrifice for willful sin and paid the required penalty once and for all. Those who reject or abandon Jesus in this life are signing their eternal death certificate. He remains the only sacrifice for willful sin. In the wisdom of God, as Jesus hung on a tree, He became a curse for us.

The different categories of sins are explicit in scripture. Though deliberate rebellion against God is worse than a fault, Jesus toned for both. He was the vicarious sufferer whose wounds, bruises, and chastisement took away all types of sins. In his repentance Psalm, David recognizes the uniqueness of each type of sin and the importance of confessing both before God.

Have mercy upon me, O God, according to thy lovingkindness: according unto the multitude of thy tender mercies blot out my transgressions. Wash me throughly from mine iniquity, and cleanse me from my sin. For I acknowledge my transgressions: and my sin is ever before me. Ps 51:1-3

Whether it were the sins of transgression or iniquity, the shed blood of Jesus was the propitiation of our sins and the sins of the whole world (1 Jn. 2:2).

In John 13, the author deliberately shifts between highlighting the actions of Peter and those of Judas. Their acts equate to the two main categories of sin. Peter's denial of Jesus was not a deliberate, intentional sin. He truly believed that he would go all the way and die for Jesus. Although his spirit was willing, his flesh was too weak (Matt 26:41). In the end, he denied Jesus and went out and wept bitterly (Matt 26:75). Judas was calculating. Satan put the betrayal of Jesus in His heart. During the earthly ministry of Jesus, Judas was an adversary among the disciples:

Jesus answered them, *"Did I not choose you, the twelve, and one of you is a devil?"* Jn 6:70

While I was with them in the world, I kept them in thy name: those that thou gavest me I have kept, and none of them is lost, but the son of perdition; that the scripture might be fulfilled. Jn 17:12

But when his disciples saw it, they had indignation, saying, To what purpose is this waste? ⁹ For this ointment might have been sold for much, and given to the poor. Matt 26:8-9

But one of his disciples, Judas Iscariot, who was later to betray him, objected, "Why wasn't this perfume sold and the money given to the poor? It was worth a year's wages." He did not say this because he cared about the poor but because he was a thief; as keeper of the money bag, he used to help himself to what was put into it. Jn 12:4-6

When Judas, who had betrayed him, saw that Jesus was condemned, he was seized with remorse and returned the thirty pieces of silver to the chief priests and the elders. "I have sinned," he said, "for I have betrayed innocent blood." "What is that to us?" they replied. "That's your responsibility." So Judas threw the money into the temple and left. Then he went away and hanged himself. Matt 27:3-5

Jesus called Judas a devil because he was constantly oppositional, fault finding, and complaining. He got upset when someone used their expensive oil to bless Jesus and tried to mask his sin by saying the money could have been used to help the poor. But John noted that he was not concerned for the poor, or what the woman did wrong. He was a thief and was treasurer for their evangelistic team. His intentional sin cost him his life. Judas hung himself and his soul was eternally damned. He was the only one of the 12 disciples called Apostles that Jesus lost (17:12)

Comparing the Sins of Peter and Judas	
Peter	Judas
Sin of Iniquity	*Sin of Transgression*
• Prone to Unintentional Mistake	• Prone to Intentional Rebellion
• Loved Jesus	• Used Jesus for Personal Gain
• Accepted Correction	• Rebelled Against Correction
• Waited for opportunity to prove loyalty	• Waited for Opportunity to betray Jesus
• Responded to open rebuke	• Ignored silent appeal to change
• Serious about ministry of Jesus	• Put money before ministry
• Repented of his betrayal and wept bitterly	• Succumbed to consequences of his sin and hung himself

Both Peter and Judas hurt Jesus, and though their sins were different, Jesus loved them "to the end." Judas chose to go through with betrayal after Jesus gave him a chance to come clean during the feet-washing moment.

Do you know what I have done to you? [13] *You call me Teacher and Lord, and you say well, for so I am.* [14] *If I then, your Lord and Teacher, have washed your feet, you also ought to wash one another's feet.* **Jn 13:12-14**

Jesus asked the disciples if they knew what He was doing for them because His actions went beyond cleaning their physical feet. He was modeling how to get to the "heart of the matter" of loving each other. Their dirty feet were symbolic of sin that, like dirt, accumulates on us but not necessarily in us. Judas had sin in him. Sin on or around us is a matter of temptation, but sin in us is a matter of condemnation. Every disciple of Jesus will accumulate daily dirt (sin on them). But no disciple should allow dirty sin to remain in their heart or soul. In washing even Judas' feet, Jesus modeled endless love for those who hurt him.

Jesus knew that Judas would sell Him out and Peter would not hold out, but He washed their feet, anyway. To be like Jesus, we must help each other clean off daily dirt so we can stay clean in a dirty, sinful world. At any given time, believers will accumulate some dirt when we sin and hurt each other. But we must not allow the hurt to become a more significant issue. We must help each other keep the dirt off. Yes, even those who hurt us need help themselves. As God's word tells us, much sin can be covered and eliminated if believers medicate with the word of truth.

PRESCRIPTION 11 - MEDITATION MEDICATION: COVER OTHERS *AND CONFESS FAULTS.*

Confess your faults one to another, and pray one for another, that ye may be healed. The effectual fervent prayer of a righteous man availeth much. Jas 5:16

Blessed is the one whose transgressions are forgiven, whose sins are covered. Ps 32:1

let him know that he who turns a sinner from the error of his way will save a soul from death and cover a multitude of sins. Jas 5:20

Brethren, if a man is overtaken in any trespass, you who are spiritual restore such a one in a spirit of gentleness, considering yourself lest you also be tempted. Gal 6:1

If we say that we have fellowship with him, and walk in darkness, we lie, and do not the truth: But if we walk in the light, as he is in the light, we have fellowship one with another, and the blood of Jesus Christ his Son cleanseth us from all sin. 1 Jn 1:6-7

Both Peter and Judas sinned and hurt Jesus. Yet, the devil was able to enter the heart of Judas (13:27) because Judas had already allowed himself to be influenced by Satan's suggestion that he betray Jesus. (13:2). Judas sin was in his heart and he did not recover. Unlike his fellow disciple, Peter's faith suffered, but he recovered from his mistake. He only needed his feet washed because he never allowed the devil access to his heart.

The risk of maintaining church hurt in our hearts is that it leads to festering anger and bitterness. Such unsettled anger gives the devil a place in our hearts to latch on to. Later referring to sin, Jesus noted to Satan:

> *I will no longer talk much with you, for the ruler of this world is coming, and he has nothing in Me.* Jn 14:30

Satan found no dirt on or in Jesus. In contrast, Judas was defiled from within because sin was rooted in His heart. The devil is able to exploit sin that resides in a person's heart, using it as a foothold to bring about their downfall. Once sin is present, the enemy can wait for the opportune moment to reveal it and cause harm. For instance, while anger itself isn't always sinful, if it's not dealt with properly, it can give the devil an opportunity to influence a person's actions and ultimately their life. That's why scripture gives clear guidance on how to handle anger—advising us to resolve it before the day ends, so it doesn't take hold.

> *Be ye angry, and sin not: let not the sun go down upon your wrath: Neither give place to the devil.* Eph 4:26-27

Anger that does not have a limit is a place for the devil to operate in a person's life. Since the devil is an opportunist, he will calculate when and how he uses anger festering in the human heart. Yes, people do suffer hurts in the realms of the church community. But it worsens when their hurt turns into anger against the offending party and the church institution. Nothing good can come from anger that festers over a period. It's not possible to get better by being bitter. Also, the anger that remains is terrible for one's physical health as well as one's spiritual health. There is a balm in the church for the hurt that turns into perpetual anger.

Because of sin in his heart, Judas needed more than his feet washed. He needed a complete conversion: a change of heart. Unfortunately, He was lost forever because he rejected Christ's love for internal sin festering in his heart.

LOVE LIKE JESUS: THE NEW COMMANDMENT

"Teacher, which is the great commandment in the law?" Jesus said to him, "'You shall love the LORD your God with all your heart, with all your soul, and with all your mind.' This is the first and great commandment. And the second is like it: You shall love your neighbor as yourself.' On these two commandments hang all the Law and the Prophets." Matt 22:36-40

A new commandment I give unto you, That ye love one another; as I have loved you, that ye also love one another. By this shall all men know that ye are my disciples, if ye have love one to another. Jn 13:34-35

As the Father hath loved me, so have I loved you: continue ye in my love. If ye keep my commandments, ye shall abide in my love; even as I have kept my Father's commandments, and abide in his love. These things have I spoken unto you, that my joy might remain in you, and that your joy might be full. This is my commandment, That ye love one another,

114

as I have loved you. Greater love hath no man than this, that a man lay
down his life for his friends. Jn 15:9-13

The word translated as *friend* is "*philos*' meaning brother. It also means an associate. The word translated neighbor in the second great commandment is a derivative of the Greek word "*pelas.*" It means one that is close and near. A neighbor does not have to be an intimately close friend but could be anyone you encounter. A neighbor can be as general as a fellow citizen and as specific as the person living next door. Also, a neighbor is anyone near another in need, as Jesus noted in the account of the compassionate Samaritan who helped a stranger in distress when two others refused to help him.

Which of these three do you think was a neighbor to the man who fell
into the hands of robbers?" The expert in the law replied, "The one who
had mercy on him." Jesus told him, "Go and do likewise. Lk 10:36-37

Jesus considered a neighbor to be anyone needing compassionate help. But the friend-neighbor to die for is an associate and a brother (sister). They do not have to be a biological sibling, but any person who does the will of God, as Jesus stated when His family was concerned about Him.

Then one said unto him, Behold, thy mother and thy brethren stand
without, desiring to speak with thee. But he answered and said unto him
that told him, Who is my mother? and who are my brethren? And he
stretched forth his hand toward his disciples, and said, Behold my mother
and my brethren! For whosoever shall do the will of my Father which is
in heaven, the same is my brother, and sister, and mother. Matt 12:47-50

Laying down one's life for a friend (ministry) is a love that is greater than loving your neighbor as yourself. In this context, the friend to lay down one's life for is a neighbor (associate, brother); but not every neighbor is a brother (associate). When the neighbor is an associate in the case of a fellow disciple, the new commandment is to be applied. Love one another as I have loved you (Jn 15:12). Jesus also referred to the new commandment as "my commandment."

The message of serving His disciples through the common task of washing their feet reaches a climax in the above statement, "Love one another as I have loved you." Through washing their feet, Jesus gives this new commandment in the same conversation and demonstration of love. Note Jesus referred to this as a new commandment. This commandment is "Love thy neighbor as thyself" raised to a higher standard. I can love my neighbor as myself and not die for them. But when that neighbor is another disciple, Jesus raises the love bar to another level. Not only do I love them as myself, but I must also love them the way Jesus demonstrated love for his disciples. Loving other disciples as Jesus Loved them is "Loving to the End." This love is sacrificial, and not hindered or hampered by offenses that are sure to occur in the body of Christ. Loving like Jesus is dying to self so that another can live.

To love other disciples as Jesus loves them is to love them regardless of how they treat you. Jesus knew that Judas was a devil and was dirty all over, but He did not expose Judas to the rest. Jesus kept loving Peter, who had faults and would deny Him the same night he insisted that he was ready

116

to die for Him. Jesus keeps loving those who hurt Him through denial and betrayal: two extremes and everyone in between. Peter allowed Satan to use His mouth (Matt 16:23), but Judas was a devil (Jn 6:70) (adversarial) who allowed Satan to enter his heart. Jesus loves them both to the end.

Love: Still two commands, not three.

A new command I give you: Love one another. As I have loved you, so you must love one another. By this everyone will know that you are my disciples, if you love one another. Jn 13:34-35

Jesus spoke these words when He was about to separate from His disciples due to His arrest. It's a new commandment but not a third one because all disciples are potential neighbors. But what makes this a new commandment within the two commandments is this: Not every neighbor is a disciple. When it comes to neighbors who are not disciples, disciples are commanded to love them as we love ourselves. But when it comes to **neighbors who are disciples**: we are to love them as we love ourselves. In addition to loving a neighbor as we love ourselves, we are to love one another as Christ loved us. When talking to disciples who are neighbors, Jesus says this is how you love one another. Also, this is how the world will know that you are my disciples: The new command brings the two greatest commandments to their highest possible expression. Jesus said no love is greater than the love that causes one to lay down His own life for a friend (brother, associate).

But what makes this a new commandment? The word translated new has to do with substance or quality: It's still loving your neighbor, but the quality of loving your neighbor has been upgraded to include an expression of love that did not exist before Jesus spent over three years with the disciples, He called Apostles. Yes, we love our neighbors as ourselves, but when the neighbors are other disciples, we also are commanded to love our neighbor the way Christ loved his 12 apostles when he was on earth. It is new because Jesus is about to do the one thing that had never been done in the history of humanity. While we were yet sinners Christ died for us (Rom 5:1-5)

THE LORD'S LOVE: THE CHURCH HURT ANTIDOTE

Therefore, having been justified by faith, we have peace with God through our Lord Jesus Christ, through whom also we have access by faith into this grace in which we stand, and rejoice in hope of the glory of God. And not only that, but we also glory in tribulations, knowing that tribulation produces perseverance; and perseverance, character; and character, hope. Now hope does not disappoint, because the love of God has been poured out in our hearts by the Holy Spirit who was given to us. Rom 5:1-5

For when we were still without strength, in due time Christ died for the ungodly. For scarcely for a righteous man will one die; yet perhaps for a good man someone would even dare to die. [8] But God demonstrates His own love toward us, in that while we were still sinners, Christ died for us. Much more then, having now been justified by His blood, we shall be saved from wrath through Him. For if when we were enemies we were reconciled to God through the death of His Son, much more, having been reconciled, we shall be saved by His life. Rom 5:6-10

Loving God and loving neighbor was as old as the Pentateuch. However, for his disciples, Jesus upgraded l loving your neighbor as yourself to loving them "the way I have loved you." Jesus' love for his disciples is the model for the church and the antidote for church hurt. His love is surreal, selfless, and sacrificial.

Surreal Love
The Lord's love was unbelievable and unheard of, like a good dream that comes true. Jesus knew that Judas was plotting to betray him, but it did not change the way Jesus treated Him. Jesus knew that Judas was dirty inside, but he still washed His feet as an expression of love.

Jesus saith to him, He that is washed needed not save to wash his feet but is clean every whit: and ye are clean, but not all. [11] For he knew who should betray him; therefore, said he, Ye are not all clean. Jn 13:10-11

Nothing Judas did changed the way Jesus treated Him. Judas came to the dinner that night, and the devil had already put it in his heart to betray Jesus. Yet Jesus offered Judas a sop, and instead of Judas repenting after that final gesture of love, the devil entered His heart. At that moment, Jesus said to him, *"what you do, do it quickly."* Judas was subject to the outcome of the scripture: because he had already agreed to sell out Jesus for thirty pieces of silver. Speaking prophetically of the betrayer, the Psalmist said:

119

Yea, mine own familiar friend, in whom I trusted, which did eat of my bread, hath lifted up his heel against me. Ps 41:9

A *familiar friend* is a safe or peaceful friend. The adversary will target those who should be safe and trustworthy and use them to hurt us. The hurt of a *familiar friend* is a deep hurt!

We love our neighbor as ourselves by having mercy on them when the situation calls for mercy. But if our neighbors betray us, we are not obligated to treat them like valued members. But when that neighbor is a disciple, we disciples treat them with Jesus's surreal love toward Judas. Judas was dirty, but Jesus never stopped offering him the cleansing power of His love. When we know that another disciple is dirty and a sellout, other disciples must love them to the end. This obligation means when our neighbor is another disciple. We've never done all that we can do for them until we have done all that Christ would have done for them, even if it's Judas. Judas is full of the devil and betrays Jesus with a kiss, and Jesus continues to treat him with kindness. This love is unheard of, but that's the love that disciples are to demonstrate in their relationship.

We are to love other disciples as Christ loved us *not as we love ourselves!* Jesus loving Judas this way means that a disciple can plot and plan against another disciple, but the victim is to continue to treat them the way Jesus treated Judas. Jesus knew it would not end well for Judas because Judas was betraying Him. He never stopped expressing loving-kindness toward Judas by showing him special attention. If one disciple is intentionally out to injure or betray another, the victim of betrayal is to respond like Jesus. Jesus loved Judas to the end, but in the end, Judas hung himself. But Jesus did not put the rope around his neck, nor was Jesus relieved that Judas kept rejecting his love until it cost him his life. Through his treatment of Judas, Jesus tells all disciples to never give up on another disciple. We must love other disciples to the very end. The same way that Jesus loved us. If an atheist or my enemy is hurt and I can help them, I must love my neighbor as myself. But if that same Buddhist or atheist vehemently rejects my kindness toward them, I'm not obligated to keep trying. It would not be wrong to keep trying, but the extra effort is not an obligation. But if that neighbor is a fellow disciple, I am commanded never to stop trying, no matter how they treat me.

Selfless Love

And He took bread, gave thanks and broke it, and gave it to them, saying, "This is My body which is given for you (selfless); do this in remembrance of Me." Likewise He also took the cup after supper, saying, "This cup is the new covenant in My blood, which is shed for you (selfless). But behold, the hand of My betrayer is with Me on the table. And truly the Son of Man goes as it has been determined, but woe to that man by whom He is betrayed!" Lk 22:19-22

The commandment is new because it is selfless love. Everything Jesus did was an expression of selfless love, especially toward Judas. Woe is an expression of pity and grief. Jesus is expressing grief over the one who was to betray Him. When we love other disciples this way, our hearts break when they do things to us that will injure themselves. Jesus knew that Judas was doing something incredibly selfish and would cost him his life. By this time, Judas had a pattern of selfishness. Judas became upset when Mary used the expensive oil that she earned to wash the feet of Jesus.

But one of His disciples, Judas Iscariot, Simon's son, who would betray Him, said, "Why was this fragrant oil not sold for three hundred denarii and given to the poor?" This he said, not that he cared for the poor, but because he was a thief, and had the money box; and he used to take what was put in it. But Jesus said, "Let her alone; she has kept this for the day of My burial. For the poor you have with you always, but Me you do not have always." Jn 12:4-8

Jesus was selfless when he did not allow His disciples to follow Him on a path that would take them through suffering, pain, and a brutal crucifixion where they would die. Their fate would have been His had Jesus freed them to fight for Him. Yet he loved His disciples "to the end" because He did not let them follow Him to the cross. But Peter was bold enough to ask Jesus why.

Peter said to Him, "Lord, why can I not follow You now? I will lay down my life for Your sake." Jesus answered him, "Will you lay down your life for My sake? Most assuredly, I say to you, the rooster shall not crow till you have denied Me three times. Jn 13:37-38

Peter denied Jesus three times as Jesus said he would. But in our scripture lessons, the resurrected Christ is showing a selfless love for Peter by offering Peter the opportunity to love him by feeding his sheep. Jesus did not hold his denial against him. Jesus ensured that now that your life is no longer in danger from following me, I will allow you to follow me. But selflessly, Jesus protected them from all he would go through for them and the Word. Jesus allowing Peter to deny him was a selfless act. Ironically it saved Peter's life because Peter proved that he was ready to fight and die for Jesus until he realized that Jesus was not fighting a physical fight. But Jesus was fighting a fight that Peter was not able or ready to fight. In his sovereign and selfless way, Jesus allowed Peter's love for his Lord to hurt him so that he would back off and not fight the wrong fight. This commandment is new because it is selfless and divine. Later this converted Peter writes:

> *Therefore, since Christ suffered for us in the flesh, arm yourselves also with the same mind, for he who has suffered in the flesh has ceased from sin,* 1 Ptr 4:1

> *For to this you were called, because Christ also suffered for us, leaving us an example, that you should follow His steps: "Who committed no sin, Nor was deceit found in His mouth"; who, when He was reviled, did not revile in return; when He suffered, He did not threaten, but committed Himself to Him who judges righteously; who Himself bore our sins in His own body on the tree, that we, having died to sins, might live for righteousness—by whose stripes you were healed. For you were like sheep going astray but have now returned to the Shepherd and Overseer of your souls.* 1 Ptr 2:21-25

This commandment is new because there is *some self* even in the command to love your neighbor as yourself. But when that neighbor is a disciple, we are to love that neighbor the way Christ put us first: the selfless way Christ loved us. He stepped into our skin to save us from our sins, then went to hell in our place and came back to life so that death would lose its grip on our souls. The command to love people to our death was unheard of, and it is still unheard of outside of the command of Jesus. There was nothing like this before Jesus demonstrated this love, and there hasn't been anything like it since Jesus expressed this love for us. The gospel's good news has made it possible for this love to be expressed among the new creation community in union with Christ. Apostle Paul expressed it this way:

> *For when we were still without strength, in due time Christ died for the ungodly. ⁷ For scarcely for a righteous man will one die; yet perhaps for a good man someone would even dare to die. ⁸ But God demonstrates His own love toward us, in that while we were still sinners, Christ died for us.* Rom 5:6-8

This commandment is new because disciples must love other disciples with this same selfless love. To the church at Philippi Apostle Paul says:

> *Let nothing be done through selfish ambition or conceit, but in lowliness of mind let each esteem others better than himself. ⁴ Let each of you look out not only for his own interests, but also for the interests of others. The Humbled and Exalted Christ⁵ Let this mind be in you, which was also in Christ Jesus,* Phil 2:3-5

When it comes to neighbors who are not disciples, we love them as we love ourselves. But when that neighbor is a disciple, we love them the way Christ loves us. This love is an unheard-of love and a higher calling because the interest of others becomes more important than our interests. But this is how Christ loved us. He put our interests before his own so that we could have eternal life. When I love my neighbor as myself, I'm still thinking about myself. But when my neighbor is a fellow disciple, I love my neighbor the selfless way Christ loved me.

Judas betrayed Jesus, but all the time, Jesus expressed love toward Judas by pulling him close. On the other hand, Peter denied Jesus, but all the time, Jesus was getting Peter out of harm's way. Protecting Peter from harm kept him safe so that he could become all that God had purposed him to be. Jesus was protecting Peter by allowing Peter to deny him three times.

Sacrificial Love

But God demonstrates His own love toward us, in that while we were still sinners, Christ died for us. Rom 5:8

Jesus went out of his way to become the sacrificial lamb to save us from our sins. When we love other disciples the way Christ loved us, we go way out of our way to show concern for them—making sacrifices to demonstrate our love to the end, even to the point of our lives. How other disciples treat us is not the basis for how we treat them. The way Christ loved us is the basis for how we treat other disciples. The Apostle Paul was one disciple who understood this commandment's gravity.

For if we are beside ourselves, it is for God; or if we are of sound mind, it is for you. For the love of Christ compels us, because we judge thus:

125

that if One died for all, then all died; and He died for all, that those who live should live no longer for themselves, but for Him who died for them and rose again. Therefore, from now on, we regard no one according to the flesh. Even though we have known Christ according to the flesh, yet now we know Him thus no longer. Therefore, if anyone is in Christ, he is a new creation; old things have passed away; behold, all things have become new. 2 Cor 5:13-17

When we love other disciples the way Jesus loved us, we sacrifice our comfort and convenience if that's what it takes to stay in accord with each other. We will do what's best for them even if it hurts them in the short term because we are looking out for them in the long term. Denying Jesus was painful for Peter. But he used the experience to help and strengthen other believers. Jesus knew that Peter was talking the talk but would not be able to walk the walk. Yet he protected Peter from himself. Protecting or covering each other is how disciples are to love each other. Even when we know that another disciple will not live up to what they are saying, when they fail, we do not treat them as though it's the end of their world and ours.

We love other disciples the way Jesus loves them when we allow them to fail us, hurt us, and deny us, but because we know that with all their bloopers and blunders, they have divinely given potential. Like Jesus, we create opportunities for them to get back up and keep moving with our support. Early the same night Judas betrayed Jesus, he had an opportunity to choose a different path as Jesus washed his feet. Jesus loved Judas to the end. In the end, Judas chose to hang himself. But Jesus did not put the noose around his neck, nor should His disciples. The believer's charge is to have the mind of Christ: "Father forgive them for they do not know what they are doing." While dying on the cross, Jesus covers His killers with a prayer of forgiveness. Don't forget that Jesus raises the bar of forgiveness to no limitation or expiration date for those of the new creation community.

Then Peter came to Him and said, "Lord, how often shall my brother sin against me, and I forgive him? Up to seven times?" Jesus said to him, "I do not say to you, up to seven times, but up to seventy times seven. Matt 18:21-22

If my neighbor, who is not a disciple, fails me and continues to attack me viciously, I do not have to allow them to continue without seeking some form of protection. Apostle Paul sometimes used his citizenship and Pharisee credentials and status to escape further hurt and abuse.

As they stretched him out to flog him, Paul said to the centurion standing there, "Is it legal for you to flog a Roman citizen who hasn't even been found guilty?" Acts 22:25

But when Paul perceived that the one part were Sadducees, and the other Pharisees, he cried out in the council, Men and brethren, I am a Pharisee, the son of a Pharisee: of the hope and resurrection of the dead I am called in question. Acts 23:6

But when that neighbor is a disciple, I am commanded to love them the way Christ loved his disciples. Loving like Christ means that when another disciple hurts me, it is not a reason to cry church hurt; instead, it is an opportunity to express the kind of love that Christ has for us. The command to love other disciples this way is a charge to follow, not a choice response. This commandment is new because it is unheard of, and nothing is like it apart from divine love.

The way Christ loved us is the solution and response for every kind of hurt that can happen to us in and out of the church. The devil is ok with the term unbiblical responses to church hurt because then we are ignoring the new commandment that Jesus gave us to solve the old selfish attitude of making my feelings the god over faith in God. Those who *"believe in God must believe God"* when hurt in the context of ministry.

> *But when you do good and suffer, if you tolerate it, this is commendable before God. For to this you were called, because Christ also suffered for us, leaving us an example, that you should follow His steps: "Who committed no sin, Nor was deceit found in His mouth"; who, when He was reviled, did not revile in return; when He suffered, He did not threaten, but committed Himself to Him who judges righteously* 1 Ptr 2:20-23

Loving to the end like Jesus is to do whatever is possible to reconcile with those who have done us wrong, or we perceive to have done us wrong. Believers must never forget we have an adversary that is a master at distortion. Too often, distorting a believer's character leads to emotional injury and an untold impact on a fellowship. Character assassination can lead to an untraceable number of failed opportunities to expand the ministry to the unsaved. A simple fix would be to quickly go to the person to get clarity because, as stated, the devil is a master at hunting in the dark. To say, "I thought," or "I felt," after months, even years of hurt and injury is a gross violation of the healing word of God that gives explicit instruction on how to handle offenses in the body of Christ. I encourage anyone still grappling with an experience of church hurt to start medicating today by meditating on the word of Truth. The medication guide in the index summarizes the scriptures mentioned in the eleven Meditation Medication Prescriptions. The blood of Jesus never loses its power. Yes, the blood still works, but only those who work the blood will enjoy the benefit of being cleansed from all unrighteousness: regardless of what others may do to hurt or injure us.

CONCLUSION

To be saved is to be Spirit-filled, which means to have a completely new Spirit agreeing with the human spirit that we are children of God (Rom. 8:16). Children of God can love like God loves because His Spirit (seed of God) is within them (1 Jn 3:9). The new Spirit and new circumcised heart are the fulfillment of God's promises: he repeatedly gives from Moses to Jeremiah to the time Ezekiel is in Babylonian Exile (Deut. 10:16, 30:6, Jer. 4:4, Ez. 11:19, 18:31, 36:26). God continued making the promise beyond the exile in Joel and beyond until the promised began to be fulfilled at the first post-resurrection Pentecost celebration (Joel 2:28-29, Acts 2:1-). The love of God is shed abroad in our hearts by the Holy Spirit (Rom. 5:5). Therefore, the fruit of the Spirit is love (Gal. 5:22) and full of health-providing vitamins: joy, peace, and longsuffering are at the top of the list. The ability to love and suffer long with each other is in the Holy Spirit, not something we learn. Therefore, the power to heal from church hurt is in the Holy Spirit, God's gift, living within the spirit-filled believer. In suffering a church hurt, do not grieve, or quench the Holy Spirit (Eph. 4:30, 1 Th. 5:19).

Loving other disciples as Jesus loved us is not an abstract concept for us to make it meaningful and personal. It is God's solution for injuries that occur among His people as well as the cure for a sin-infested world. Therefore, it is the foundation for resolving the idea of church hurt. God's love is existential in that it is to exist in real time and space, especially within Holy Spirit-filled believers.

Through outreach, much energy is expended and programs are put in place to show non-believers love and win them to faith. Yet Jesus told His disciples to model love for each other without limitations as a way of winning non-believers or outsiders to faith. Yes, we should show people *the love of God,* who visit our sanctuaries. But disciple-making begins with us modeling love toward insiders in the presence of outsiders. According to Jesus, outsiders will connect this behavior with our belief in Jesus. The night Jesus had this conversation about love, he prayed that His disciples would be one (Jn 13-17). This same night, He began to accomplish the death that would change humanity forever. His last will and New Testament is our guide for avoiding or overcoming the highly contagious church hurt disease.

Then I heard a loud voice saying in heaven, "Now salvation, and strength, and the kingdom of our God, and the power of His Christ have come, for the accuser of our brethren, who accused them before our God day and night, has been cast down. And they overcame him by the blood of the Lamb and by the word of their testimony, and they did not love their lives to the death. Rev 12:10-11

PRESCRIPTION 1 - PRAY & LIVIE BY SCRIPTURE

Acts 4:24-26, 5:40-42.
Leaders in the infant church prayed scripture when they were persecuted for ministering in the name of Jesus. When they were beaten for not stopping, they rejoiced for being found worthy to suffer shame for His name.

Deuteronomy 28:1-14.
Those in a covenant agreement with God can pray His word and know that they will receive the prosperous benefits of the Covenant: prosperity, health, wealth, healing, and assurance of recovery from whatever the situation may be. The only requirement is obedience to the word of God.

•

Deuteronomy 28:15-68.
Those who do not obey the voice of the Lord can expect the opposite of health and healing to occur.

•

1 Kings 8:35.
Centuries later, Solomon prayed a prayer of dedication based on God's covenant agreement with Israel, mainly found in Deuteronomy 28.

2 Chronicles 7:13-16:
God answered by reaffirming His commitment to the covenant agreement that included healing. If His people,

called by His name, would *"humble themselves, and pray, and seek my face, and turn from their wicked ways; then will I hear from heaven, and will forgive their sin, and will heal their land."*

Deuteronomy 28:36, 49.

Israel broke the covenant agreement from generation to generation until, eventually, God judged them according to the words of the covenant agreement. During the time of Jeremiah, "The Lord brought a nation against them from afar and carried them into exile.

1 Kings 8:35.

While in exile, Daniel prayed with his face toward Jerusalem (Daniel 6:10) because he remembered the prayer of Solomon that said: "When heaven is shut up, and there is no rain because they have sinned against thee; **if they pray toward this place**, and confess thy name, and turn from their sin, when thou afflictest them:

Daniel 9:2-3.

Daniel also prayed for the end of the exile based on the word of God spoken to Jeremiah (25:11-12).

1 Corinthians 11:30.

All covenants work the same. The church is in a covenant relationship with Jesus. With His stripes, we are healed from the inside out. However, when the church at Corinth broke the Covenant by hurting and mistreating each other, Apostle Paul warned about the consequences: "For this cause, many *are* **weak** and **sickly** among you, and many **sleep**." All the curses of the covenant God made with Israel can be summed up by the three words: 'weak', 'sickly,' and 'dead' (Deuteronomy 28:15-68). In the New Testament sleep is used to describe the death of believers in Jesus (Jn 11:11, 1 Thess 4:14-15).

1 Corinthians 11:29-32.

The consequences for breaking the new Covenant are the same as those for breaking the Old Covenant. Apostle Paul says many of them cut their lives short by hurting and mistreating other saints. However, because of the sacrifice of Jesus to atone for death, some lives are cut short under the New Covenant. This way, the offenders will not face condemnation with those who perish due to not being in a covenant relationship with Jesus Christ.

PRESCRIPTION 2 - BE UNITED WITH CHRIST.

John 15:4, 7, 9.

Being fully united to Christ forms a union that allows all that is available in Christ to flow into the believer's life. This union includes all the healing needs of the human soul. The analogy of fruit-bearing confirms that asking according to one's desire is restricted to what is needed to bear the necessary fruit. In this case, the fruit is love.

1 Peter 2:24.

Apostle Peter reminds the believer that the prophecies concerning the vicarious suffering savior found in Isaiah 53 were fulfilled in the selfless, sacrificial death of our Lord and savior Jesus the Messiah. By His stripes the church in general and believers in specific have healing. The Healer of hurt is the head of the church, which is His body. Using the human anatomy to describe the union is literal, not analogical. For All who would accept this truth, The church is truly the *mystical*, not *mythical*, body of Christ. The healing that is needed is built into the body itself.

Rom 6:5-11, 8:3-4.

Here Apostle Paul describes how baptism symbolizes being united with Christ in His death. The dead body of Jesus was filled with all the sins of the world. He bore the in His innocent body. The sins of humanity were buried along with the body filled with our sins. When Jesus rose, He rose to leave our sins in the grave. Those who are buried in baptism are being baptized into His death. He rose to a new resurrection life. Being united with Christ, those with the Spirit of Christ rise to live a new life. Death loses its power altogether. Those who are united to Christ are to count themselves dead to sin and alive to Christ. Jesus condemned sin in the flesh, something that the old covenant law could not do.

Philippians 2:5.

Being in union with Christ is not an automatic solution. The believer has to choose to allow the same mind that determined the actions of Christ to determine their actions as well. When it comes to being hurt in church, Having the mind of Christ is paramount. Those who are hurt in church, like Christ, must be willing to humble themselves to whatever is happening and allow God to exalt them in His time. Taking this position is not easy and may even be painful. However, we cannot begin to imagine what it felt like for Christ to go through to be the propitiation for our sins and the sins of the entire world. We do not have to shed any blood, just decide to respond with humility.

PRESCRIPTION 3 – ATTEMPT TO RESOLVE ALL CONFLICTS

1 John 1:6-7.

Maintaining fellowship with God is walking in the light (living according to scripture). Those who do not live a lie by suggesting they are in fellowship with Him. This fellowship is the foundation of believers being in fellowship with each other: a fellowship that allows the blood of Jesus to cleanse all unrighteousness from among the church.

Matthew 18:15-17.

Resolving conflict among believers is a 4 step process about exhausting all possible means before giving up on the possibility of reconciliation. It is critical to note what is not said. The fellowship is part of the process of reconciliation. The community is to be together to shame the offender into reconsidering the need to seek forgiveness. Nowhere in scripture is it implied that an offended person should use the hurt as a reason to leave the fellowship.

Mark 11:25-26; Matt 5:23-24.
Addressing faults is to occur before praying to God. If not, the offended risk not being forgiven for their trespasses. If a hurt believer knows that the one who hurt them did it intentionally because they have something against them: they are to make the first step in seeking reconciliation. The hurt saints are not to bring a gift to God before trying to resolve the conflict. Obeying the commands of Jesus, who is light, is the meaning of walking in the light.

2 Corinthians 2:10-11.
If a refusal to try to resolve conflict is due to unforgiveness, Satan has a reason to gain an advantage in the fellowship of the saints. Any level of division allows Satan to spread even more darkness and the power of darkness (Lk 22:53). Darkness is the adversary's stronghold. Like a roaring lion, Satan seeks an opportunity to devour the vulnerable. Lions' favorite hunting time is at night, for it is difficult for their prey to see and escape. The adversary is unbeatable in the darkness because he has the advantage. Only light can dispel darkness. A willingness to forgive is walking in the light.

Ephesians 6:11.

The word of God is the believer's offensive weapon in the armor of God. The Word of God is the sword of the Spirit, not the sword of the believer. The believer must not grieve or quench the Holy Spirit (Eph. 4:30, 1 Thes. 5:19) living inside them. When a believer is hurt in the church for any reason, the Spirit of God inside them uses God's word to shed light and dispel darkness. Unresolved conflict among believers are like a blackout in the church.

2 Corinthians 5:18-19.

Reconciliation is at the heart of the Christian messages. It would be nonsense for ministers of reconciliation to refuse to exhaust all efforts to resolve conflict and reconcile.

1 John 1:9; James 5:16.

Confessing sins to each other is another way to clear the air of darkness and resolve conflicts. Confessing trespasses couples with praying for each other is putting medication on the injury. The supplicating prayer is an effective healer.

PRESCRIPTION 4 - BE A PRISONER OF THE LORD

Acts 9:4-5, 15-16.

Apostle Paul's example is a case study in understanding how being hurt in ministry is integral to discipleship. Jesus stopped Saul from continuing his quest to eliminate those calling Jesus Lord and Christ. Instead of punishing Him,

Jesus put him in the ministry. At that time, Jesus revealed to Him that suffering great things for His name's sake would define his ministry.

Philippians 3:12-18.

In a letter written from prison, Apostle Paul is at peace knowing that Jesus apprehended Him and pressing on to attain why he was apprehended was a primary goal. He welcomed and even yearned to experience the suffering that Jesus suffered if it would deepen his fellowship with Jesus.

Philemon 1:1; Ephesians 4:1, 6:19-20.

Apostle Paul saw himself as a prisoner of the Lord. He saw himself as belonging to the Lord as a prisoner. Realizing that what he deserved was death for slaughtering innocent people: being a suffering prisoner of the Lord was a welcomed privilege and blessing for him. As an ambassador in chains, he was ready to fearlessly declare the gospel, regardless of the hurt that he was experiencing.

1 Timothy 1:12-16.

Apostle Paul realized that he was a blasphemer and persecutor who had hurt others, and Jesus showed him mercy because he was acting in ignorance. Yes, he was suffering, but the Lord was longsuffering with Him. Belonging to the Lord was sufficient to help him absorb being hurt by others. He was ready to put his life on the line for Christ, who had shown him great mercy.

PRESCRIPTION 5 – ACCEPTING GOD'S WILL AS THE ONLY WAY TO EXPERIENCE HURT

Acts 2:22-23.

While filled with the Holy Spirit, Peter cites that although the religious leaders wickedly crucified Jesus, the entire charade was within the determinate counsel of God. Jesus was aware that He was doing God's will, which gave Him the ability to suffer physical, mental, and emotional hurt at the hands of those claiming to represent God.

Luke 22:40-46.

Jesus positioned Himself in the place to be arrested, knowing that the pain and suffering would be unlike anyone had ever experienced before. He only desired the cup to be taken away if it was the will of God. But He was willing to endure the ordeal if that was the only way to accomplish his Father's will.

John 18:10-11; Matthew 26:52-54.

Peter was ready to suffer and die with and for Jesus, but Jesus would not allow Him to do so. Also, Jesus revealed that more than 72,000 angels were already mobilized, and all He had to do was ask His Father for their assistance.

Luke 22:50-53.

Jesus questions the chief Priest for using the cover of night to arrest Him with a mob as if He was a dangerous person. He exposed the darkness of their soul when He pointed out that they intentionally used the cover of darkness because of the power of darkness.

1 Thessalonians 5:16-19.
Because Jesus allowed the joy that awaited Him to drive His decision to go through the will of God: the spirit-filled believer has the ability Always to rejoice, pray without ceasing, and give God thanks no matter what is occurring. Whatever is occurring will be the will of God in Christ Jesus concerning the Christian: including being hurt in the church.

PRESCRIPTION 6 – THINK RIGHT ABOUT BEING WRONGED BY OTHERS

Philippians 2:5-8.
Believers are to let the mind of Christ determine the way we process suffering. He was equal with God yet humbled Himself down to the cross's death—all the time, trusting God for His vindication and exaltation.

John 15:18-21; Matthew16:24-25. Disciples must consider that a servant cannot be greater than their master. Jesus was hated first. Therefore being hated in the world is in line. Although the aggressor is the world here, the message would be the same regardless of the source of the hurt. Anyone who comes after Jesus must be willing to deny themselves and bear a cross: symbolic of suffering pain.

Romans 5:1-5, 8:35-37; Psalms 44:22.

Believers now stand in a place of grace, where they can glory in tribulation, knowing that tribulation is part of the ministry of hope due to the love of God being poured out into one's heart. When one ponders the depth of the love of Christ, their mind would be set on not allowing anything to separate them from this love even though, as the Psalmist said, we are counted as sheep to the slaughter all day long. Instead of being a victim, we are more than conquerors.

Gal 2:20.

Believers are thinking right when they see themselves crucified with Christ and are now living by the faith of the Son of God who loved us and gave His life for us. As the Apostle Paul says, now the believer lives by the faith of the son of God.

2 Corinthians 4:8-10.

Although various attacks surround believers: living the dying of the Lord Jesus is what is occurring, not a reason to pity oneself.

Philippians 3:10-11.

Explaining His willingness to humble himself, Apostle Paul desired to know Jesus in the power of His resurrection, which meant that he would first have to share in the fellowship of His suffering. The right way to think would be to welcome suffering for the cause of Christ to receive the benefit of being drawn even closer to Christ and what He experienced.

1 Peter 4:1 Hebrews 5:8-9.
Peter reminds those who think suffering is strange but a reason to rejoice because they are participating in the Lord's suffering. Again, regardless of the source of the suffering, whether in the church world or the world outside the church, although Jesus was a son, He learned obedience through the things He suffered. The suffering Christ experienced was at the hands of Jews and Gentiles, religious and nonreligious. By doing so, He became the author of eternal salvation and the faith that we now live.

PRESCRIPTION 7 - MEDICINE FROM HEAVEN FOR HEALING ON EARTH

1 Peter 1:18-19, Isa 52:14, Acts 20:28.
Jesus came down from heaven with the precious blood of God running through His veins. As the sacrificial lamb of God, he painfully shed that blood through the marred opens in His flesh. For all who believe in Jesus, the blood still works on past, present, and future hurts. God purchased the church with the blood of Jesus.

Jeremiah 8:20-22.
Jeremiah noted in his day that even though medicine was available, the people could not heal because they refused to

take it: the word of truth. Those under the new Covenant must not make the same mistake. Under the New Covenant in the blood of Jesus, the church has all the medicine it needs to heal all hurts. "With His stripes, we are healed (present tense."

Matthew9:11-12; John 5:43, 6:35-38.
Jesus identified His mission as that of a physician sent to heal the sick. He is the bread of life and the thirst quencher for souls dehydrated due to a spiritual drought. He is on earth solely to do the Father's will. Sin sickness is due to human rebellion, but the sin-infested sickness of the soul is far from the Father's will for humanity.

John 9:39, 10:10, 12:46. Jesus came to give sight to the blind and make blind those who can see (exposing the truth about those who refuse to see.) But those who believe in Him will not remain in darkness. He is the light and life. He alone has come to dispel the three-fold agenda of the enemy to steal, kill, and destroy.

•

John 18:37. When Pilate asked Jesus if He was a king, Jesus confirmed He was. But he explained that He is a different kind of King. Truth is His message, and those who respond to truth confirm they are part of His kingdom. Although Paul did not understand His answer, Pilate was convinced that Jesus was no threat to the state of Rome.

Luke 2:30-32; Matthew 1:21. Simeon was one in a general population of despondent Jews waiting for the consolation of Israel. Although the Jews were physically out of Babylonian captivity, they were still in bondage due to their sin. Jesus came to save His people from their sins. When Simeon looked at the baby Jesus, he knew he was looking at the salvation of Israel.

PRESCRIPTION 8 - CORRECTLY DIAGNOSING THE HURT

O Jerusalem, Jerusalem, thou that killest the prophets, and stonest them which are sent unto thee, how often would I have gathered thy children together, even as a hen gathereth her chickens under her wings, and ye would not! Behold, your house is left unto you desolate. For I say unto you, Ye shall not see me henceforth, till ye shall say, Blessed is he that cometh in the name of the Lord. Matt 23:37-39.

As Jesus wept over the condition of Jerusalem and its pending doom, He pointed to their constant rebelling against and killing the prophecy who kept bringing the word of God for their recovery from sin.

John 12:20-27.
As the time grew closer for Jesus to suffer and die, he was not looking forward to it, but He that His hold reason for existing on earth came down to this significant event.

Beyond this event, His death would open the door for all nations to return to God through believing in Jesus. His popularity was already spilling over into other groups, and Jesus knew that it meant that He had first to die and resurrect for the ministry to expand beyond the walls of the present religious society (mainly Judaism).

Hebrews 12:2-3.

Although Jesus despised the shame of crucifixion, he knew that the joy it would bring was reason enough to go through with it. The joy and hope for humanity were nonexistent until Jesus got to the root cause of all hurt: sin. As a vicarious sufferer, He took all our grief, transgressions, iniquities, and lack of peace and bore them in His body to make permanent healing available. He diagnosed the human condition as sin in all its expressions and manifestations. What is seen as church hurt falls within the list of many that His stripes can heal. Those with ears must hear what the Spirit is saying to the church. The root cause is sin, and the prognosis is the sacrificial death of the lamb of God.

1 Peter 2:21-24.

Christ is our example of responding to what causes us to hurt and suffer. Instead of allowing it to linger and spread as church hurt, the hurting must follow His steps. He did not sin, and nothing wrong came out of His mouth. He did not fight back but committed His way to God, the righteous judge. He admonishes others to do the same things because healing hurt is through all He experienced for us.

PRESCRIPTION 9 - MEDITATION MEDICATION: LOVE THE TRUTH OF GOD'S WORD.

Jeremiah 23:32, 29:8; 2 Tim 4:3-5.

During the time of Jeremiah, the people embraced the lies propagated through false prophets, so they refused the balm brought to them by God through Jeremiah. Sadly enough, they did not recover from their rebellion against the spoken words through the God-sent prophet Jeremiah. God noted that the false dreams resulted from the people's desires to hear what sounded good versus the medicine that was good for their recovery from the disease of sin. Under the New Covenant, the Apostle Paul noted that the end times would be when something similar would occur. Some will refuse to tolerate sound doctrine but will instead embrace those who will tell them what they want to hear and not what is necessary for maintaining spiritual health.

> *The coming of the lawless one is according to the working of Satan, with all power, signs, and lying wonders, and with all unrighteous deception among those who perish, because they did not receive the love of the truth, that they might be saved. And for this reason, God will send them strong delusion, that they should believe the lie, that they all may be condemned who did not believe the truth but had pleasure in unrighteousness.*
> 2 Thess 2:9-12;

Exodus 4:21. Apostle Paul reveals to this church those who do not already have a love for the truth will be vulnerable to deception. The coming of the lawless one will be filled with deceptive acts that will cause some to perish (as it did in the time of Jeremiah). Not receiving love for the truth is the inditement. Even more, there will be a point of no return. God will send a strong delusion that they will believe a lie. Recall God hardened the heart of Pharaoh not from a pure heart, but His heart was hard when God sent Moses to him. Sending a strong delusion is like God strengthening the heart of Pharaoh. Again, Pharaoh's heart was already hard. God simply hardened it after several years of His terrible treatment of the Hebrew people.

PRESCRIPTION 10 - MEDITATION MEDICATION: APPLY LOVE THAT HEALS WHILE IT HURTS

Ezekiel 36:26-27 (11:19)
Through Ezekiel, God promises a new heart and a new spirit as a form of a heart transplant that would cure them of the sin of disobedience. God made this promise while they were devasted for being exiled into Babylonian captivity.

Romans 5:1-5; Galatians 5:22-25.
The promise is fulfilled when God pours His love into one's heart. It is the work of the Holy Spirit (the promised new Spirit that makes a new (healed) soul. The fruit of the Holy Spirit is love. In love some vitamins make the new soul

healthy and protected from the hurt that kills. The love of God is an effective vaccine against the virus of sin.

Ephesians 4:30-32, Matthew 5:43-48.

To ensure that healing can flow, the believer must not grieve the Holy Spirit, for He is the seal until full redemption is realized. Spirit-filled individuals have the power to put away bitterness, wrath, anger, clamor, and evil, speaking with all malice. They can be kind, tenderhearted, and forgiving. to one another. Believers who allow the Holy Spirit to work in their new hearts can love their enemies, bless those who curse them, do good to those who hate them, and pray for those who spitefully use and persecute them. [45] that you may be sons of the Father in heaven.

Romans 5:6-8; John 14:15; 1 John 4:20-21.

Jesus demonstrated God's love that sustains the believer and heals even from deep pain. He showed this love when we were at our weakest and unable to help ourselves. Christ gave His life for us while we were still far from God, demonstrating a love that reaches us in our brokenness. In the same way, we shouldn't wait until we feel worthy or strong to follow His command to love others, no matter our emotions. Our willingness to obey this commandment is evidence of our love for the Lord. For in loving our brother and sister, we show our love for God. Further, it is impossible to truly love God without also loving fellow believers.

John 4:24.

God is Spirit, and His kind of love can only be fully experienced by those who have received a new heart and spirit. Therefore, Spirit-filled believers must surrender to the Holy Spirit, allowing Him to express His unconditional love through us— even when the flesh wars against it.

PRESCRIPTION 11 - MEDITATION MEDICATION: COVER OTHERS AND CONFESS SINS

James 5:16.

Confessing sin and praying for one another leads to healing.

Psalms 32:1.

Those who rebel can still be forgiven and those whose mistakes are forgiven are blessed, people.

James 5:20; Galatian 6:1.

The effort to rid a person of sin saves a soul and covers a multitude of sins that could and would occur. So the spiritual person must lead the way in restoring anyone overtaken in sin using an ingredient (vitamin) found in the fruit of love: gentleness.

1 John 1:6-7

Maintaining fellowship is paramount. The only way it is possible is for believers to walk according to the word of

God so that the blood of Jesus can keep cleansing the body of Christ of all sin.

Notes

As we all grow old, and facts become obscured and fables are told. Let these real accounts of God's divine providence, protection, and provision testify to the future generations that Jesus Christ is the same yesterday, today and forever.

Konnie Parson

www.ingramcontent.com/pod-product-compliance
Lightning Source LLC
Chambersburg PA
CBHW071400120626
46546CB00002B/760